Taunton's

BUILD LIKE A PRO®
EXPERT ADVICE FROM START TO FINISH

Installing Floors

Joseph Truini

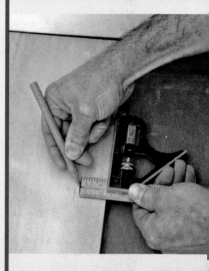

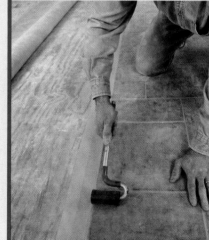

The Taunton Press

To Marla, for her many years of unwavering love and support. To Kate and Chris, my heart and soul.

The Taunton Press
Inspiration for hands-on living®

The Taunton Press, Inc., 63 South Main Street, P.O. Box 5506, Newtown, CT 06470-5506
e-mail: tp@taunton.com
EDITOR: Jennifer Renjilian Morris
COPY EDITOR: Seth Reichgott
INDEXER: Lynda Stannard
COVER DESIGN: Kimberly Adis
INTERIOR DESIGN: Lori Wendin
LAYOUT: Cathy Cassidy
ILLUSTRATOR: Mario Ferro
PHOTOGRAPHER: Geoffrey Gross, except where noted

Library of Congress Cataloging-in-Publication Data

Truini, Joseph.
  Installing floors / Joseph Truini.
     p. cm.
  Includes index.
  ISBN 978-1-60085-112-4
  1. Floors--Installation. 2. Flooring--Installation. I. Title.
  TH2521.T83 2010
  694'.2--dc22

                        2010007752

Printed in the United States of America
10 9 8 7 6 5 4 3 2 1

Construction is inherently dangerous. Using hand or power tools improperly or ignoring safety practices can lead to permanent injury or even death. Don't try to perform operations you learn about here (or elsewhere) unless you're certain they are safe for you. If something about an operation doesn't feel right, don't do it. Look for another way. We want you to enjoy working on your home, so please keep safety foremost in your mind.

ACKNOWLEDGMENTS

First, thank you to all the talented people at The Taunton Press. In particular, thanks to Helen Albert, who first offered me this book. Thanks, too, to book editor Jennifer Renjilian Morris for smoothly transforming my mess of electronic files and images into a well-organized book. In the course of writing a book as complex as this, there are a million little—and not so little—questions and concerns that crop up throughout the writing process. Without a trusted ally, none of these details would've gotten resolved. So I'd like to express my gratitude to editorial assistant Jessica DiDonato for her many months of invaluable and incredibly helpful assistance.

I was once again lucky enough to work with photographer extraordinaire Geoffrey Gross, whose keen eye and even keener sense of humor made each shoot day seem like a holiday.

I couldn't have produced this book without the generosity of the homeowners and contractors who welcomed me into their homes and jobsites. Thanks to Jimmy Tiganella of Classic Tile in Oakville, Connecticut, for the craftsmanship and immeasurable patience displayed during the installation of the glazed-porcelain, marble, and vinyl tile floors.

Thanks to Dr. John Way, owner of Private Eye Vision in New Milford, Connecticut, for

allowing us into his home to shoot the bamboo floor, which was installed by Tom Wenzel of Wenzel Contracting, South Kent, Connecticut.

I'd like to thank Erik Rydingsword of Franklin Hardwood Floors, Woodbury, Connecticut, for letting us photograph the oak-strip floor, and for introducing me to Tom Pelletier of Flooring America, also in Woodbury. Tom, in turn, introduced me to installer Marcel Binette, who expertly and patiently showed me how to lay laminate planks. And thanks, too, to Tarkett® field sales rep Jason Farabow for his expert technical assistance during the installation of the vinyl sheet floor.

I'd like to express my sincere thanks to the following folks who went out of their way to provide me with information, photographs, and technical data: Troy Brown (Lyptus® by Weyerhaeuser), Samantha Frost (Pergo®), Shane Smartt and Terri Todd (Kährs®), Joseph Hozer and Pier Antoine Marier (DuroDesign), Harriet Ayoade (Mannington®), Laurie Kirk-Rolley (DalTile®), and Ann Knight (Teragren® Fine Bamboo).

Last, I'd like to recognize Dena Ferrell of Kährs, whose friendly, helpful demeanor and infectious spirit won her many admirers; she'll be missed by all who knew her.

CONTENTS

INTRODUCTION

Back in 1985, I installed a radical new type of "floating" hardwood floor from Sweden that was unlike anything I—or most anyone else in the United States—had ever seen before. It was called laminated flooring because each plank was composed of thin wood layers that were glued—or laminated—together. The top layers of the long tongue-and-groove planks were covered in ⅛-in.-thick hardwood strips. (This type of flooring is now called engineered wood to differentiate it from plastic-laminate flooring.)

I installed the flooring in the living room at my parents' home, and even wrote an article about it for *Popular Mechanics* magazine. And although I didn't know it at the time, that Swedish import helped revolutionize the flooring industry and kick off an explosion of do-it-yourself flooring products.

Over the years, engineered wood became more popular and easier to install, and soon other DIY-friendly flooring products started to appear, including snap-together laminate planks and tiles, floating vinyl sheets, cork-veneered planks, prefinished solid bamboo, even tape-down carpet squares.

The result of all this upheaval—and billions of dollars in research, design,

and manufacturing—is that professional contractors no longer dominate floor installations. Today, there are dozens of floors that are specifically designed and packaged for do-it-yourself homeowners. And the widespread use—and rental—of pneumatic tools has even made traditional nail-down floors accessible to DIYers.

The goal of this book is to introduce you to the many fabulous flooring products now available, but more important, I want to give you the confidence and inspiration to tackle your own flooring project. To help you understand the installations, you'll find detailed drawings, hundreds of step-by-step photographs, and accompanying text that describes each step of the process.

My work on this book is done, but I feel as if there's some unfinished business. I know for a fact that every major flooring manufacturer is feverishly working on the next greatest generation of better, greener, easier-to-install flooring. And although I don't know what to expect, each time I visit my mom and see that 1985 floating floor, I can't help but think that the final chapter has not yet been written.

WIDE WORLD OF FLOORING

There's no doubt that we demand more from our floors than from any other building material in our home. We tromp across them with muddy boots and piercing heels, scrub them with soapy water, drag furniture across them, and assault them with clawing pets and kids in cleats. Yet we expect our floors to withstand this daily onslaught and remain in like-new condition for years.

The good news is that many of today's flooring materials not only meet our real-world expectations, but often exceed them. In this section we'll examine a wide variety of flooring options, which have been divided into six main categories: wood, tile and stone, laminate, resilient vinyl, bamboo, and cork. Within each category are many variations, styles, and colors of flooring, so I'm sure you'll discover at least a few that'll serve admirably in your home for years to come. ▶ ▶ ▶

(Photo at left courtesy Kährs)

To protect a wood floor, be sure to

- Sweep and vacuum regularly to remove dirt and sand that can scratch the finish.

- Place mats or rugs at all entrances for wiping your shoes.

- Put protective glides on furniture legs.

- Avoid flooding the floor with water, and immediately clean up all spills.

- Never drag furniture or appliances across the floor.

Most solid-wood

flooring is manufactured with a moisture content between 6 and 9 percent. Place unopened packages of flooring in the room at least three days prior to installation, so the wood can acclimate to the air temperature and humidity.

Wood Flooring

You've got two basic choices when it comes to wood flooring: solid wood or engineered wood. And each of those types comes unfinished or prefinished. The flooring you'll ultimately choose will depend on several factors, including price, wood species, ease of installation, the type of subfloor, and the room itself.

Solid-wood flooring

Solid-wood flooring has been popular ever since dirt-floored Colonial-era cabins gave way to more proper homes. Even today, houses with wood floors sell faster and fetch higher prices than homes without them. Solid-wood flooring offers a multitude of design and finishing options, comes in many species, and is easily repaired and refinished. Plus, a properly maintained wood floor can easily last several generations.

Solid-wood flooring is readily available in both unfinished and prefinished varieties. Traditional unfinished hardwood-strip flooring is the most popular wood floor installed today. It's affordable and attractive, and you can choose to stain it any color you'd like or to leave it natural. However, unfinished wood requires sand-

A mixture of several exotic hardwoods, including Brazilian walnut, teak, and eucalyptus, are used in this solid-wood floor from Mohawk® Flooring. Called Jakarta, it features ³⁄₈-in.-thick by 3-in.-wide floorboards that can be glued or nailed down. (Photo courtesy Mohawk Flooring)

ing, staining (if desired), and the application of a clear topcoat finish.

Prefinished wood flooring costs more than unfinished flooring, but it's growing in popularity because it doesn't require sanding or finishing. As soon as the last plank is installed, you can nail up the baseboard and carry in the furniture. Prefinished flooring also comes in thinner planks

Wood Flooring: DIY Finish vs. Prefinished Flooring

PREFINISHED FLOORING has a lot going for it: It reduces installation time by several days and keeps dust and odors out of the house. Finishes are sprayed on and heat-cured in dust-free, factory-controlled settings. They include UV-protected and aluminum-oxide formulas that typically outlast a site-applied finish.

However, do-it-yourself finishing is still preferred in many cases because it allows you to choose the exact stain color and number of topcoats to apply. Plus, unfinished flooring costs considerably less than prefinished flooring, even when you take into account the cost of sanding and finishing.

The natural warmth and beauty of Southern long-leaf heart pine is on full display in this traditional pine floor by Carlisle Wide Plank^SM Floors. The planks come in widths up to 10 in., and feature tight vertical grain that's nearly as hard as oak. (Photo courtesy Carlisle Wide Plank Floors.)

than unfinished flooring, which creates less trouble when transitioning from one room to the next.

Solid-wood flooring is suitable for virtually any room in the house, but it's best to avoid moisture-prone areas, such as bathrooms and laundries. It also shouldn't be used in below-grade situations, such as basements and other underground rooms.

Putting wood floors in kitchens has been a popular trend for the past decade or so, especially in homes with open floor plans where the kitchen, dining room, and adjacent hallway all flow together. To protect the floor from the inevitable stains, splashes, wear spots, and dents, lay water-resistant carpet runners in front of the counters and refrigerator. Another option is to install a distressed floor; its rustic appearance will hide minor blemishes.

Wood flooring is commonly available in narrow strips, wide planks, and parquet squares. Traditional 2¼-in.-wide oak strip is by far the most popular type, but 5-in.- to 6-in.-wide planks are more common than ever before, especially in large rooms, such as living rooms, dens, and great rooms. Parquet flooring comes in preassembled tiles or can be custom made from individual strips of wood. Parquet is ideal for creating eye-catching geometric patterns, weaves, and herringbones.

In recent years, hand-scraped, rustic, and classic Old World looks have become commonplace. Deeper, richer colors—cinnamon, toffee, and caramel—are popular, too. Exotic woods with unusual grain patterns and colors continue to appeal to many homeowners.

Wood is a renewable resource, but some species take so long to grow and are being harvested so quickly they're no longer considered sustainable. The best way to ensure that you're buying responsibly harvested wood is to confirm that the flooring is certified by the Forest Stewardship Council or a similar environmental agency.

Engineered-wood flooring

Prefinished engineered-wood flooring was introduced to North America in the mid-1980s and quickly became the most popular type of do-it-yourself wood floor. It's composed of three or more wood layers that are glued together into long planks. The top layer is a thin solid-wood veneer, which comes in nearly two-dozen species. Laminated construction creates a floor that's much more dimensionally stable than solid-wood flooring, so it's less likely to cup, split, shrink, or warp.

WHAT CAN GO WRONG

Solid-wood flooring isn't recommended for moisture-prone areas, such as basements, baths, and laundry rooms, or for spaces with very high humidity. Moisture can cause wood flooring to swell, cup, and buckle, even if the proper expansion space exists around the room's perimeter.

TRADE SECRET

Solid-wood flooring is available in a variety of grades. Oak and ash, for example, are available in clear (no knots), select (small knots and minor color variations), and common grades 1 and 2 (more knots and greater color variation). All grades are sound, but each will give a different look, from formal to rustic. Price, too, is affected by grades, with clearer flooring costing more.

Engineered-wood flooring is also less suscep-tible to damage from moisture than solid wood. It can be installed virtually anywhere, including below-grade rooms and directly over a concrete slab. However, it's important to lay the flooring over the appropriate underlayment. Check with the flooring manufacturer to ensure you're using the correct underlayment for the subfloor or slab.

Most engineered-wood planks measure between 3 in. and 7 in. wide and 7 ft. and 8 ft. long, and come in thicknesses ranging from about ⅜ in. to ¾ in. It's worth mentioning that

Engineered-wood flooring comes in many exotic wood species that aren't available in any other type of floor. This strikingly hand-some wide-plank floor is made by Kährs from kosipo, an exotic that's denser than maple, oak, ash, or cherry.

although a vast majority of engineered-wood flooring comes prefinished, in some parts of the country you can find unfinished planks.

When shopping for engineered-wood flooring, make sure the top veneer is at least ⅛ in. thick, which will allow sanding and refinishing, if necessary. You'll also notice that the flooring comes in three basic styles: one-, two-, and three-strip planks. Those designations refer to the number of veneer strips visible in the top layer. A one-strip plank resembles a single, wide board. A two-strip plank looks like two narrow floorboards. The three-strip plank most closely mimics a traditional hardwood-strip floor; each plank appears to be three narrow boards.

The planks have tongue-and-groove joints milled along all edges and ends. The reason DIYers love engineered-wood flooring is that the planks snap together and "float" over a thin underlayment. There's no nailing or gluing, so installation is quick and neat. Plus, the planks can be laid directly over an existing floor, as long as it's hard, flat, and in sound condition.

Tile and Stone

Although they're not the easiest to install, tile and stone products create arguably the most beautiful and durable of all floors. Man-made tiles fall into two basic categories: ceramic and

porcelain. Natural stone tiles are exactly that: slabs of stone cut from the earth and shaped into floor tiles. Which of these masonry products you should install will depend on the particular style you're trying to create with regard to tile size, color, pattern, and texture. However, also consider hardness, overall cost, installation ease, and stain and slip resistance.

Glazed ceramic tile

Glazed ceramic tile is one of the most functional and decorative of all building materials. Made from a mixture of mined clays and other natural minerals, the tiles are shaped, topped with a glaze, and fired in a kiln. The result is a hard, flat, easy-to-clean surface that's impervious to staining.

This remodeled bath features a classic mosaic-tile floor composed of 1-in.-sq. glazed ceramic tiles. These American Olean® satin-white and gloss-black tiles come in 12-in. by 12-in. sheets for easy installation; style shown: Signature Classics Chloe, Number CH02. (Photo courtesy American Olean)

A floating engineered-wood floor is a good choice for installation over radiant-heat tubing. It's not as susceptible to temperature and humidity as solid-wood flooring, so it's less likely to warp or buckle. However, be sure to keep the heat temperature below the maximum recommended by the flooring manufacturer.

TRADE SECRET

It's best to order all ceramic or porcelain tile needed for a room at the same time. That'll be your best chance of getting all the tiles from the same lot number. Tiles from different lots are often slightly darker or lighter in color.

SAFETY FIRST

When choosing ceramic or porcelain tile for wet areas, opt for matte finishes and slightly roughened textures, which will help prevent slipping. It's also smart to use nonslip mats near sinks, tubs, and showers to avoid accidental falls.

Rich, dark brown floors are typically made of stained wood, but this dining room is surfaced with American Olean 12-in. by 12-in. glazed-ceramic tile; style shown: Signature Classics Broadway Brown, Number PK04. (Photo courtesy American Olean)

Testing Tile Toughness

WHEN CHOOSING A GLAZED porcelain tile, check its surface hardness rating to ensure it'll stand up in your home. The test developed by the Porcelain Enamel Institute (PEI) rates tiles from 0 to 5. The higher the number, the more abrasion resistant the tile is.

- PEI 0: Not recommended for floors
- PEI 1: Light traffic
- PEI 2: Medium traffic
- PEI 3: Medium-heavy traffic
- PEI 4: Heavy traffic
- PEI 5: Extra-heavy traffic

Note: Some tiles are rated for hardness according to the MOHS test, which is based on a scale from 1 to 10, with 10 having the hardness of diamond. For residential floors, a rating of at least 5 will ensure excellent wear resistance.

Unglazed ceramic, such as terra cotta tile, is also available, but it must be treated with a clear sealer to protect its porous surface.

The body of ceramic tile is typically white or reddish in color. If you drop something hard onto the floor and chip the glazed surface, the body color will show through. Of course, that's not a problem with unglazed tiles, which are solid color throughout.

Ceramic tile is popular in areas that get wet on a regular basis, including kitchens, bathrooms, laundries, and foyers. It's also ideal over radiant heat because it absorbs and releases heat slowly and evenly over long periods of time. And tile is a good choice for allergy sufferers because it doesn't support allergens and it can easily be scrubbed clean.

Porcelain tile

Like ceramic tile, porcelain tile is available in both glazed and unglazed varieties. Unglazed porcelain tiles are commonly referred to as color-body tiles, meaning that the surface color is uniform throughout the tile. However, porcelain tiles are made from ultra-fine porcelain clays and fired at much hotter temperatures than ceramic tiles. As a result, they're much harder, more dense, and less porous than ceramic tile. Porcelain tiles are also less likely to crack, have superior resistance to moisture and staining, and can be installed indoors or outdoors. For all these reasons and others, most professional tile contractors prefer porcelain floor tiles to ceramic tiles.

When shopping for porcelain tile, you'll see many styles that are dead ringers for natural stone products, especially marble. Now, it's hard to beat the natural beauty of real stone, but a stone-pattern porcelain tile doesn't have any of the imperfections and weak spots inherent in

natural stone. So you end up with a floor that looks like stone but is much more durable and easier to clean.

There are also porcelain-tile planks that look like weathered wooden boards, right down to the wood-grain texture.

Natural stone

Granite, slate, marble, travertine, and limestone are just some of the natural stones that are available as floor tile. Again, there are manmade tiles that mimic stone and most even cost less, but for discriminating homeowners who value authenticity, it's hard to beat the natural beauty, texture, and color of real stone.

Natural stone is fairly expensive, so it's best to install it where it'll have the greatest impact, such as in a foyer or master bathroom. Preassembled

This interesting floor pattern is composed of DalTile's 12-in. by 24-in. color-body porcelain tiles set between 2-in. by 24-in. tiles of the same color. The design on the tiles is reminiscent of fine silk or linen. (Photo courtesy DalTile)

WHAT CAN GO WRONG

Natural stone tiles often vary slightly in thickness, even in tiles taken from the same box. This may necessitate a deeper mortar bed than anticipated and affect how you'll handle transitions. Check each box and remove any tiles that are much thicker or thinner than the average.

Natural slate is one of the most dense and durable of all natural-stone floors. Here, gray-black 12-in. by 12-in. American Olean slate creates a subtle yet sophisticated floor. Note that light-gray grout was used to outline and highlight each tile. (Photo courtesy American Olean)

This stunning natural-stone floor, by DalTile, features large square sections of tumbled-stone tiles framed by an eye-catching mosaic border (above). The 6-in.-wide border is composed of tiny tumbled-stone tiles set in a woven serpentine design (inset). (Photo courtesy DalTile)

stone medallions and borders are also available, which can be used in a ceramic or porcelain tile floor to create an attractive focal point.

Stone tile is installed very much like ceramic or porcelain tile. It's typically set in thinset mortar over a substrate of plywood or cement backerboard. The spaces between the tiles are then filled with grout. The biggest difference is that you can't cut stone with a manual score-and-snap tile cutter. You must use a motorized wet saw, which you can rent by the day. The saw employs a toothless, diamond-impregnated blade and water bath to easily slice through the stone.

A properly installed stone-tile floor will last for many generations, but it's not impervious to everything. In fact, natural stone is rather porous, so it isn't very stain or moisture resistant. That's why it's important to apply the recommended sealer at least once a year to the entire surface and twice a year in bathrooms and other heavily used rooms. To reduce scratches, regularly sweep and vacuum the tile, and place mats or rugs at doorways to collect dirt.

Laminate

When laminate flooring was first introduced to North America from Europe in the mid-1990s, it was a mere curiosity. Some thought, a joke. Well no one's laughing now. Laminate flooring is the fastest-growing flooring sold today and is available from more than a dozen manufacturers. It also happens to be extremely easy to install, making it a favorite amongst do-it-yourselfers.

The flooring is composed of a dense fiber-board core topped with a layer of plastic laminate, which is similar to Formica® and other laminates used on kitchen countertops, with one important difference: The high-pressure laminate used for flooring is 20 times harder than

countertop laminate. Consequently, laminate flooring is highly scratch and dent resistant, very durable, and extremely easy to clean.

Laminate flooring comes in both long planks and square tiles; each type has tongue-and-groove joints that snap together to create a floating floor. The flooring is installed over a thin underlayment; no glue or nails are required. Some premium laminate products come with a factory-applied underlayment already adhered to the underside of the flooring, thus saving you from having to install a separate underlayment.

Wood-look planks are without question the most popular type of laminate flooring. You can find laminate planks that mimic nearly every known hardwood and softwood species, including oak, maple, walnut, pine, cherry, teak, and even bamboo and sea grass. And they come in a rainbow of "stained" colors ranging from sun-bleached white to midnight ebony. The planks measure 5 in. to 7 in. wide and nearly 4 ft. long.

A Look inside Laminate Flooring

LAMINATE FLOORING IS BUILT UP of several layers of resin, paper, and fiberboard to produce an inexpensive alternative to more expensive wood, stone, and tile floors. The bottom, or backing, is typically of melamine plastic. It offers stability and moisture resistance and is bonded to a core layer of high-density fiberboard. The decorative top layer is bonded to the core and is usually printed from a high-resolution photograph. The decorative layer is protected by a wear layer, which typically contains aluminum oxide and resin.

And, like engineered-wood flooring, laminate planks come in three basic styles: one-, two-, and three-strip planks.

TRADE SECRET

When shopping for laminate planks, be sure to check the thickness of the planks. Generally, the thicker the plank, the better the flooring, and the easier it is to install.

Looking well worn from years of foot traffic, this easy-to-install plank floor will maintain its aged appearance for years to come because it's actually a plastic-laminate floor from Pergo's American Cottage Collection. Style shown: Boathouse Pine. (Photo courtesy Pergo)

Laminate tiles are typically about 15 in. sq. and available in a wide variety of colors and textures that resemble stone, brick, and glazed ceramic tile. Many premium products even feature recessed grout lines to further fool the eye.

Laminate flooring is best suited for living rooms, family rooms, and bedrooms. Some types can be installed in moisture-prone areas, such as kitchens and bathrooms, but they'll require extraordinary care and vigilance. It's imperative to keep water from penetrating seams or getting under the flooring, and all spills and splashes must be sopped up immediately.

Resilient Vinyl

Despite the widespread demand for hardwood, laminate, and ceramic-tile floors, resilient vinyl remains extremely popular. That's because vinyl is surprisingly durable, quite affordable, quick to install, easy to clean, and suitable for all rooms,

including kitchens, baths, and foyers. Recent advancements have allowed manufacturers to offer higher-quality vinyl flooring in a wider array of realistic wood-grain and tile patterns. (By the way, vinyl flooring is classified as "resilient" because it gives slightly when you step on it and then returns to its normal profile.) Here's a detailed look at three basic types of resilient vinyl: sheet, tiles, and planks.

Vinyl sheet

Like many other flooring products, vinyl sheet has evolved to become much more DIY friendly. In fact, it's one of the easiest of all floors to install. At one time, vinyl sheet flooring had to be glued down to the entire subfloor with sticky mastic. Then, perimeter-bonded vinyl was introduced; you only had to apply glue around the room's perimeter. And although there are still some glue-down products, the latest generation of "floating" vinyl sheets install nearly as easily as a throw rug. It's not fastened down to the subfloor in any manner.

Very few flooring products come in as many colors and patterns as vinyl sheet. There are literally several dozen styles to choose from, including ones that resemble hardwood planks, glazed ceramic tile, natural stone, slate, and brick. Plus, there's an array of solid colors to consider, including checkerboard and stripes.

Another distinct benefit of vinyl sheet flooring is that it comes in many different-size patterns—squares, rectangles, octagons, diamonds—allowing you to pick one that best suits the room. Typically, flooring with smaller patterns, such as 2-in.-sq. tiles, look best in smaller rooms, and larger patterns work best in more spacious rooms.

Vinyl sheet flooring is available in 12-ft.-wide rolls, which can be cut to virtually any length. That means seamless coverage in most rooms, but you can seam together two pieces, if necessary. Shopping for vinyl sheet flooring can be a bit tricky. Prices vary widely from one flooring to the next, even though they look exactly the same. The difference is most often based on the construction of the flooring; some are just better made than others.

Fortunately, all major manufacturers offer several lines of vinyl sheet flooring, ranging from good to better to best. Higher-quality products cost more but are also thicker and more durable, and have longer warranties. So, when comparing vinyl sheet flooring, be sure to check not only the price, but also the manufacturer's warranty.

TRADE SECRET

Unroll vinyl sheet flooring and allow it to "relax" for an hour or so prior to installation. That'll give the flooring time to flatten out, which will make installation easier.

The subtle color, grain pattern, and texture of natural slate tiles are captured in this Tarkett FiberFloor® vinyl sheet flooring; style shown: Canyon Slate Brown Moss. (Photo courtesy Tarkett Fiber Floors)

Two types of Mannington Adura® vinyl flooring were used to create this eye-catching design. Sicilian Stone beige quartz tiles are divided into squares by strips of Spalted Georgian Maple planks. (Photo courtesy Mannington Adura)

PROTIP

Vinyl tiles and planks are more supple and easier to install when the weather is warm. If you're installing the floor during cold weather, turn up the heat in the room.

Vinyl tiles

Vinyl tiles aren't nearly as popular as vinyl sheets, but they're still a good choice for many DIY installations. The 12-in. by 12-in. tiles are easy to handle, cut, and install, and they can be used in virtually any room, including kitchens, baths, laundry rooms, and even basements and garages.

There are primarily two types of vinyl tiles: self stick and dry back. Self-stick tiles come with a pressure-sensitive adhesive applied to the back of each tile. You simply peel off the backing sheet and press the tile to the subfloor. Dry-back tiles must be set in a special adhesive that you have to trowel down onto the subfloor. It takes more time and effort to install dry-back tiles, but you end up with a more permanent, harder-wearing floor.

Vinyl tiles come in a variety of solid colors and in many patterns that resemble natural stone. The advantage of using vinyl tiles as opposed to vinyl sheets is that you can easily mix and match tiles of different colors and patterns to create a custom floor.

When shopping for vinyl tiles you'll find them divided into three basic groups: printed vinyl, solid vinyl, and vinyl composite. Printed vinyl is comprised of layers; it comes in a greater number of colors and patterns. However, solid vinyl and vinyl composite tiles are harder and more durable, and feature the same color throughout from top to bottom. Again, let the price and manufacturer's warranty help you identify the highest-quality products.

Vinyl planks

The newest type of resilient flooring, vinyl planks, provides the look of hardwood flooring in a super-thin, easy-to-install vinyl strip. As with vinyl tiles, vinyl planks come in both self-stick and glue-down varieties.

The planks measure approximately 3 in. to 5 in. wide and 36 in. to 48 in. long. It requires quite a bit of work to install vinyl planks in large spaces, so this product is best suited for hallways and small bedrooms and dens. (If you want the benefits of vinyl and the look of wood in a large room, consider vinyl sheet flooring.)

Feeling creative? Combine vinyl planks with vinyl tiles to create a custom floor of "stone" tiles bordered by "hardwood" strips. Most manufacturers have design guides that will suggest different integrated patterns.

Bamboo

The popularity of prefinished bamboo flooring continues to grow, thanks to its contemporary look and environmental advantages. Botanically speaking, bamboo is grass, not wood, so it grows incredibly fast. Most bamboo plants can be harvested in just four or five years. Even more surprising is that bamboo is harder than both oak and maple. And like hardwood flooring, bamboo can be installed in virtually any room, but it's best to avoid baths and other high-moisture spaces.

There are two basic types of bamboo flooring: engineered planks and solid bamboo planks. Engineered bamboo is similar to engineered-wood planks; it's installed using the floating-floor method. Solid bamboo is fastened with nails or staples, just like traditional hardwood flooring.

It's easy to mistake this plank floor for hand-scraped jatoba, an exotic hardwood from South America. It's actually made of 5-in.-wide vinyl planks from the Mannington Adura collection; style shown: Jatoba Roasted Pepper. (Photo courtesy Mannington Adura)

Capture the look of clear pine without sacrificing durability. These natural blond vertical-grain bamboo planks from Teragren Fine Bamboo Flooring are denser than most hardwoods and come prefinished. (Photo courtesy Teragren Fine Bamboo Flooring)

SAFETY FIRST

Bamboo is very fibrous, so it splinters very easily. Never slide your hand along the edge of a plank or you may end up with a nasty splinter.

PROTIP

Bamboo flooring
comes in dozens of colors, which you can see online and in brochures. However, the only accurate way to truly judge the color is to see it firsthand. If the flooring dealer doesn't have flooring samples available, contact the manufacturers. Most will send you a free flooring sample for review.

It's worth noting that there are three different kinds of solid bamboo flooring: vertical-grain solid strip, flat-grain solid strip, and strand bamboo. Vertical-grain bamboo is composed of thin bamboo strips that are stacked on edge and glued together butcher-block style. Flat-grain bamboo, the most common type, is made up of 15 thin, flat strips of bamboo, which are laminated together. Strand bamboo is manufactured from super-thin shredded bamboo fibers that are mixed with resins and pressed into rock-hard planks.

Bamboo flooring typically measures about $5/8$ in. thick and $3\frac{1}{2}$ in. to $7\frac{1}{2}$ in. wide. It's available in lengths ranging from 36 in. to 72 in. And although the grain pattern and natural color of bamboo are both rather subtle, bamboo flooring is available in more than 50 different colors, ranging from soft cedar tones to bright reds and greens.

Cork

Cork flooring is perhaps the most unusual and unsung of all flooring products. Cork comes from the bark of the cork oak tree, which is native to southwest Europe and northwest Africa. The bark can be harvested about every 10 years—without killing the tree—making cork a truly renewable product.

Cork makes an excellent flooring material because it's soft, warm, and comfortable underfoot, and is highly resistant to moisture and wood-boring bugs. Cork has superior sound-absorbing qualities, making it much quieter to walk on than wood, tile, laminate, or even vinyl.

Cork flooring is available in solid tiles and engineered planks, in both prefinished and unfinished varieties. The tiles measure $3/16$ in. or $5/16$ in. thick and can be 12 in. by 12 in. or 12 in. by 24 in. They're generally installed using an adhesive. Engineered cork planks are $1/2$ in. thick by 12 in. wide by 36 in. long. They have a cork veneer applied to a high-density fiberboard core. Cork planks can be floated over virtually any surface, including plywood, concrete, and many existing floors.

There's not really any room in the house where you can't install cork flooring. It's suitable for kitchens, baths, and basements. In fact, it's becoming a favorite floor for kitchens because dropped plates and drinking glasses are unlikely to break.

Cork is available in a wide variety of textures and shades, from subtle wood tones to vivid colors. And because cork flooring cuts easily, it can be used to create interesting borders, inlays, and other designs.

Cork flooring—both tiles and planks—can be easily cut and assembled into one-of-a-kind designs. Here, tiles from DuroDesign Flooring were used to create a diagonal diamond-pattern frame that mimics an area rug (above). (Photo courtesy DuroDesign)

DuroDesign Flooring offers cork tiles in more than 50 different colors. Four of those colors were used to create this cozy-soft, custom kitchen floor (left). (Photo courtesy DuroDesign)

Where Does Cork Come From?

YOU'D THINK COUNTY Cork, but no. Most cork comes from southwest Europe, especially Portugal. Once a cork oak tree reaches maturity, after about 25 years, the thick layer of bark is cut off by hand, a process that doesn't harm the tree. The rough exterior of the bark is removed and the inner portion is then ground into granules of various sizes. The cork particles are then mixed with binders, formed into large blocks, and baked. The dry, hardened blocks are then sliced into tiles, sheets, or veneers for use in the manufacture of cork flooring.

The tree's bark can be harvested every 10 years or so, and cork trees live up to 250 years, so a single tree can produce an amazing amount of cork in its lifetime.

UNFINISHED OAK STRIP

In this chapter, I'll show how to install the world's most popular type of wood floor: unfinished oak strip. That's a bit surprising when you consider that most modern wood floors are easier and quicker to install than oak strip. However, no other floor captures the natural warmth and beauty of hardwood quite like a traditional strip floor.

Here, I installed 4-in.-wide, random-length white oak strips. The solid-wood flooring measures a full ¾ in. thick and has tongue-and-groove joints milled along the edges and ends. The floorboards were laid over a thin moisture barrier and then nailed down with a pneumatic flooring nailer, which shoots specially designed nails, called power cleats. (The nailer and cleats are available at most tool-rental dealers.)

Once the flooring was installed, its surface was sanded and finished with tung oil varnish. All the specialty tools needed to sand and finish the floor can also be rented. ▸ ▸ ▸

1 Tools and Materials
p. 23

2 Prep the Room
p. 24

3 Prep the Subfloor
p. 25

4 Start Flooring
p. 27

5 Continue Flooring
p. 29

6 Complete the Installation
p. 30

7 Sand and Finish the Floor
p. 31

TRADE SECRET

To keep pneumatic nailers working smoothly, put three drops of light machine oil inside the tool's hose fitting at the start of each workday.

TRADE SECRET

Compressed air contains moisture that can eventually rust out the compressor's air-storage tank. To prevent damaging corrosion, try this: At the end of each workday, disconnect the air hose, but leave the compressor plugged in. Turn down the air pressure to about 20 lb. or 25 lb., then open the bleed valve at the bottom of the tank. As the compressor runs, it'll blow the rusty water out of the tank. Allow the compressor to run for about a minute, then turn it off, close the bleed valve, and unplug the compressor.

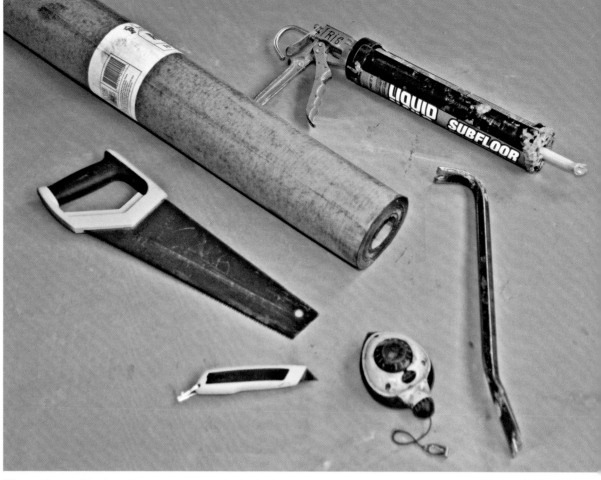

The tools used to install oak-strip flooring include the following (clockwise from the top): caulking gun with construction adhesive for adhering the first and last rows of flooring, pry bar to force floorboards into position, chalk reel for snapping a starting line, utility knife for cutting the moisture barrier, handsaw for undercutting doorjambs and casings, and roll of asphalt-saturated moisture barrier.

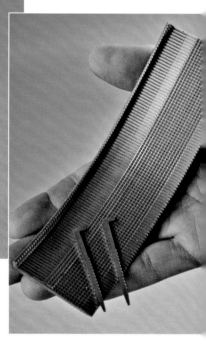

Most of the flooring is secured to the plywood subfloor with a pneumatic flooring nailer (above) that shoots 2-in.-long flat, barbed nails called power cleats (inset). To drive the cleats, use the rubber mallet to strike the poppet actuator, which is the black knob located on the top of the nailer.

Tools and Materials

You won't need many tools to install an oak-strip floor, but you will need an air compressor and two pneumatic tools: a flooring nailer to fasten the floorboards and a finishing nailer to face-nail the first and last rows. One other specialty tool that speeds up the installation is a manual flooring nailer. This compact tool is used to nail down floorboards that are situated close to walls and other areas that are too tight to accommodate the larger pneumatic flooring nailer. You'll also need a tablesaw to rip floorboards to width, and a power miter saw or jigsaw to crosscut them to length.

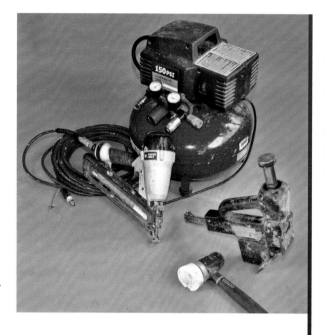

The pneumatic flooring nailer can't fasten every floorboard; it's just too big to fit into tight spaces. Therefore, you'll need an air compressor with finishing nailer (top), and a manual flooring nailer and mallet (bottom).

OAK-STRIP FLOORING OVER PLYWOOD

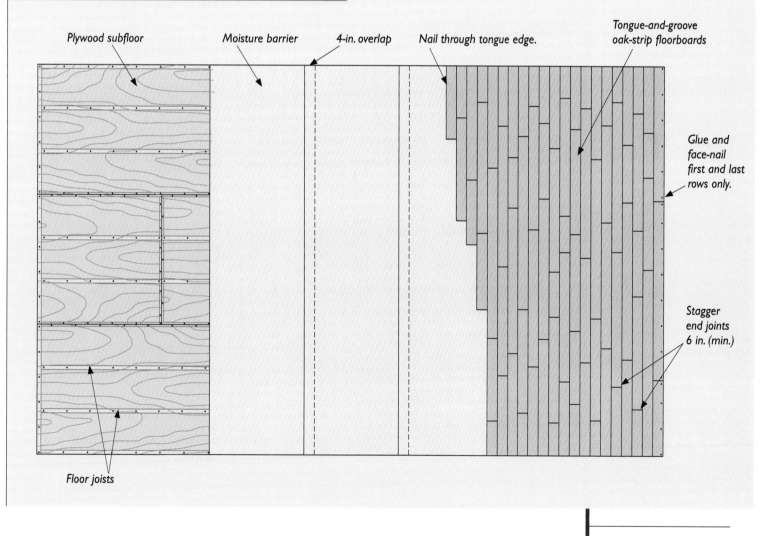

Plywood subfloor

Moisture barrier

4-in. overlap

Nail through tongue edge.

Tongue-and-groove oak-strip floorboards

Glue and face-nail first and last rows only.

Stagger end joints 6 in. (min.)

Floor joists

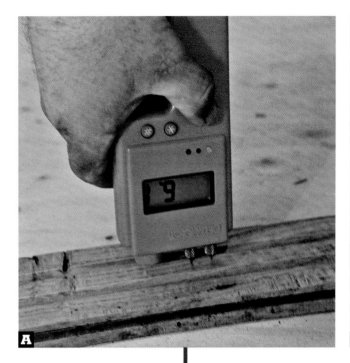

Prep the Room

The first step is to empty the room of all furniture and remove the old flooring. Because oak-strip flooring is ¾ in. thick, it's usually not feasible to lay it over an existing floor, unless it's thin vinyl. All other flooring should be removed. Thankfully, in this particular room the old carpeting had been carted away long before I showed up.

Oak-strip flooring usually comes in cardboard- or plastic-wrapped bundles. It's important to stack the bundles inside the room for three to five days prior to installation. That allows time for the wood flooring to acclimate to the room's air temperature and humidity.

Before you can begin nailing down floorboards, there are a few important steps to take to get the room ready. These steps may seem unnecessary, but they'll save you some time and trouble in the end.

1. Use a moisture meter to check the moisture content of the flooring, as shown in **A**.

Ideally it should read between 6 and 8 percent. If you install flooring with excessively high moisture, large gaps will appear between the floorboards when the wood eventually dries out. If the moisture content is very low, the floorboards could buckle when they absorb moisture and swell slightly.

Check the moisture content of the subfloor, too. It should be within 3 or 4 percentage points of the oak flooring.

2. Trim the bottoms of the doorjambs and casings to allow the new flooring to slip underneath. This is much easier than trying to notch the flooring to fit around the doorways.

Lay a floorboard upside down in front of the door casing to protect its top surface and to serve as a cutting-height guide. Set a handsaw on top of the floorboard and cut through the casing, as shown in **B**. Be sure to remove the severed wood piece and vacuum up the dust.

Prep the Subfloor

The last step before you can begin nailing down floorboards is to prepare the plywood subfloor. Start by driving 1⅝-in. drywall screws down through any subfloor areas that are loose or squeaky. Also patch any damaged spots with wood putty or floor-leveling compound. Then proceed with the installations of a moisture barrier and transition moldings.

Put down a moisture barrier

Because wood is naturally porous you must take steps to protect the flooring—as much as possible—from the adverse affects of moisture. And the first line of defense is to cover the plywood subfloor with an asphalt-saturated moisture barrier. Red rosin paper is commonly used beneath wood flooring, but asphalt-saturated paper provides better protection from moisture.

1. Roll out lengths of the 3-ft.-wide moisture barrier across the room. Cut it to fit tight from wall to wall, then unroll another piece, overlapping the first sheet by 4 in., as shown in **A**. Continue in this manner until you've covered the entire subfloor with the moisture barrier.

2. Now, determine whether you need to rip down the floorboards in the first row to ensure that the last row is at least 2 in. wide. Here's how to calculate the width of the first and last rows: Measure the room width, then divide by the width of a floorboard. That'll give you the number of full-width boards needed to cover the floor, plus the width of any remaining board. If the remaining board is less than 2 in. wide, you'll need to rip the first-row planks an appropriate amount to make the last row at least 2 in. wide.

3. At the starting wall, slide the moisture barrier back to expose about 8 in. of plywood subfloor. Measure off the wall a distance equal to the width of the first-row floorboards, then snap a chalkline parallel to the starting wall, as shown in **B**. This line represents the first row of floorboards.

4. At one end of the chalkline, near the room corner, measure from the line all the way across the floor to the ending wall. Record that dimension. Move to the opposite end of the chalkline and repeat this step, measuring across the floor to the ending wall. Compare the two measurements. If they aren't equal, then you must adjust the chalkline to ensure that it's parallel with the ending wall. This is an important step, because if you start laying floorboards that are slightly askew, the last row of flooring will be wider at one end than the other—a sure sign of shoddy work.

Install transition moldings

Transition moldings are needed around the room perimeter wherever the new oak floor will abut an adjoining room or doorway. You can buy premade moldings and thresholds, but it's just as easy to cut them from one of the oak floorboards.

1. Use a caulking gun to apply a continuous bead of construction adhesive along the subfloor in front of the doorway, as shown in **C**. If necessary, cut away the moisture barrier to expose a few inches of subfloor, and be careful not to get any of the sticky adhesive onto your shoes.

2. Set the transition molding in place and secure it with a pneumatic finishing nailer and 2-in. nails, as shown in **D**.

Start Flooring

With the subfloor prepped, it's time to begin nailing down floorboards. However, you can't use the pneumatic flooring nailer for the first row because it's too close to the wall. You'll have to fasten these boards with the finishing nailer.

Install the first row

1. Start by applying a continuous bead of construction adhesive to the subfloor, as shown in **A**. Be sure to keep the adhesive between the chalkline and wall.

2. Set the first floorboard in place right on the chalkline with its tongue edge facing out. Face-nail the board to the subfloor with 2-in. finishing nails, as shown in **B**. Space the nails about 16 in. apart.

3. If the floorboard curves away from the chalkline, use a pry bar to pull it back into alignment, then nail it through its tongue, as shown in **C**. Continue to drive nails through the tongue, spacing them 6 in. to 8 in. apart.

4. Cut the last board in the first row to length using a power miter saw. If you don't own a miter saw, use a jigsaw. And don't worry if the cut is a bit rough, as it'll be hidden by baseboard molding.

5. After installing the first row, lay out all the floorboards across the room, as shown in **D**. Set the longest boards in the middle of the room and the shorter ones near the walls. This system is much faster than walking back and forth after each row to grab floorboards off the stacks.

A

B

C

D

PROTIP

It might be a little inconvenient, but do all the cutting of floorboards outside or in an adjoining room. That way, the room where you're working will stay clean and you won't have to constantly stop to sweep up the dust and debris.

WHAT CAN GO WRONG

Be sure to use a non-
marring white rubber
mallet to strike the floorboards. If you use a standard black mallet, you'll
leave dark scuff marks
all over the flooring.

PRO TIP

You must stagger the
end joints by at least
6 in. from the previous
row, but the floor will
look much better—and
possibly even squeak
less—if you stagger the
joints 12 in. to 16 in. apart.

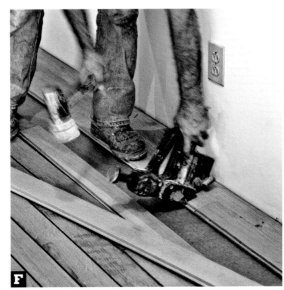

Install the second and third rows

1. Set into place the first board in the second
row, making sure it extends past any end joints
in the first row by at least 6 in. Stand with one
foot over the seam between the two boards,
which will help align the tongue-and-groove
joint. Then use a rubber flooring mallet to
pound the second-row board tightly against
the first row, as shown in **E**. It will take a little
effort, but keep hitting the floorboard and the
gap will eventually close.

2. Once the seam is tight along the entire
length of the tongue-and-groove joint, use the
manual flooring nailer to fasten the floorboard
to the subfloor. Strike the actuator knob on
the nailer with a mallet to drive the 2-in. nails
through the protruding tongue, as shown in
F. Space the nails 6 in. to 8 in. apart.

   Continue to install floorboards in the second
row, making sure you stagger the end joints by at
least 6 in. Cut the last floorboard in the row to
length using the miter saw or jigsaw, and nail it
in place.

3. Install the third row using the same techniques employed for the second row, with one
notable exception: Use the pneumatic flooring nailer, not the manual nailer, to fasten the
floorboards, as shown in **G**. It's now possible to
use the pneumatic nailer because you're working far enough away from the wall that there's
space to accommodate the larger fastener.

A

Continue Flooring

As you make your way across the room, one floorboard at a time, follow the same installation sequence used for the previous rows. When you come across a defective floorboard, which is inevitable, put it aside. Sometimes you can cut out the damaged section and use the good part of the board, or simply install the imperfect board inside a closet or other tucked-away spot.

B

1. By the time you reach the middle of the room, you'll feel much more comfortable using the pneumatic flooring nailer, and things will speed up considerably. Continue installing floorboards, making sure to pound the joints closed before nailing through the boards' tongues and into the subfloor, as shown in **A**. Again, stagger the end joints by at least 6 in. and space the nails 6 in. to 8 in. apart.

2. Occasionally the pneumatic nailer won't drive a nail all the way flush with the tongue. When that happens, stop and remedy the situation. If you don't, the protruding nail head will make it impossible to install the next row of flooring.

Hold the tip of the pry bar against the protruding nail head and strike the bar with the steel end of the flooring mallet (not the rubber end), as shown in **B**. Keep hitting the pry bar until the nail is flush with the board's tongue.

3. At some point, you'll likely have to notch a floorboard to fit around a room corner, closet, or other obstruction. Small alterations can be completed with a jigsaw, but when it's necessary to make a long, lengthwise cut into a floorboard, use a tablesaw. It's simply the fastest, most accurate way to cut the flooring.

Complete the Installation

Putting down the last couple rows of flooring is similar to installing the first few rows. You'll have to switch tools and face-nail the row closest to the wall.

1. As you approach the ending wall, you'll run out of room for the pneumatic nailer and will have to revert back to using the manual flooring nailer, as shown in **A**. Use the manual nailer to install the third- and second-to-last rows.

2. When you reach the very last row, cut back the paper moisture barrier to expose about 4 in. of subfloor. Then apply a generous amount of construction adhesive to the plywood, as shown in **B**.

   If necessary, rip the last-row floorboards down to size, making sure you cut off the tongue edge and keep the groove edge.

3. Turn the last-row floorboards upside down and use the mallet to bust off the bottom lip of the groove edge. Pull off the splintered lower

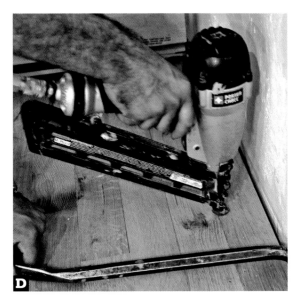

lip, as shown in **C**, leaving the upper lip intact. Removing the lower lip makes it much easier to slip the last row into place.

4. Install the last-row floorboards, using a pry bar to force the joint closed while you face-nail it to the subfloor with the finishing nailer, as shown in **D**.

Sand and Finish the Floor

At this point you're probably wondering why you didn't install a prefinished floor, but don't worry. With the proper tools and techniques, this final phase goes pretty quickly.

It usually takes about two to four hours to sand the floor in an average-size room. Then, to apply at least three coats of varnish will take one to two hours per coat, including sanding between applications. So, to sand and finish an average room will take approximately six to ten hours over the course of three or four days. Not a bad investment for a brand-new, durable hardwood floor.

Sand the surface

1. Start by filling all noticeable surface cracks and knotholes with epoxy filler, as shown in **A**. Epoxy is much harder and bonds much better than standard wood putty. Blend the two-part epoxy according to the manufacturer's directions. Then take a belt sander and sand a scrap piece of flooring. Collect the sanding dust and mix it into the epoxy so the patch will more closely match the color of the flooring. Allow the epoxy to cure until hard, which usually takes about an hour.

2. Rent an electric drum sander and sand the floor, starting with a super-coarse 40-grit sanding belt, as shown in **B**. It's very important that you sand parallel with the floorboards and in the same direction as the wood grain—not across it. Also, be sure to keep the sander in constant motion. Stop in one spot for even an instant and you'll sand a depression into the floor.

After sanding the entire floor with the 40-grit belt, switch to a slightly finer 80-grit belt and sand the floor again. Then, switch one last time to an even finer 100-grit belt and make the final sanding pass across the floor.

A

B

Each time you switch the drum-sander belt to a finer-grit abrasive, vacuum the floor clean. That way there won't be any coarse abrasive grits left behind from the previous belt to scratch up the floor.

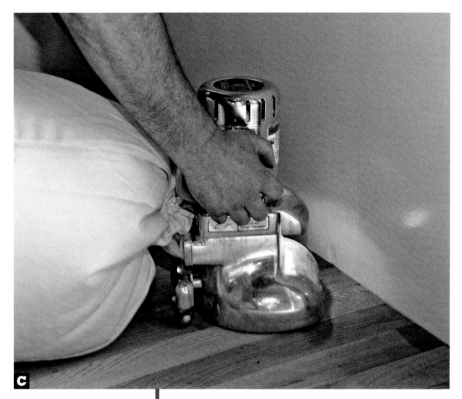

screen. Press a 120-grit screen onto the buffing pad, as shown in **D**. The weight of the machine and the coarseness of the pad will hold the screen in place.

2. Turn on the buffing machine and slowly guide it back and forth across the floor in overlapping passes, as shown in **E**. One pass over the entire floor is sufficient.

When you're done screening the surface, vacuum the floor clean.

Apply the finish

1. This oak floor was finished with a super-durable tung oil varnish. You could also use polyurethane varnish. Start by using a 4-in. paintbrush to apply varnish around the room's perimeter, as shown in **F**. Spread the varnish at least 6 in. from the walls.

2. Use a lamb's wool applicator to spread a thin, even layer of varnish over the entire floor, as shown in **G**. The raw oak floorboards will be very porous, so they'll absorb a lot of varnish. However, be careful not to leave behind any puddles.

3. Allow the varnish to dry overnight, then smooth the surface with the electric buffer fitted with a 220-grit sanding screen. Vacuum the floor clean.

3. The drum sander is a very effective tool, but it can't sand right up against the walls. To smooth the area around the room perimeter, you'll need to rent an edge sander, which uses 6-in.-dia. abrasive disks. Bolt a 100-grit disk onto the sander and very slowly work your way around the entire room perimeter, sanding the floor smooth, as shown in **C**. Don't lean too hard on the sander or you'll carve swirls into the floor. The sander is fitted with wheels, so just guide it around the room; the tool's weight will provide the right amount of pressure.

When you've finished sanding, vacuum the floor clean.

Screen the floor

1. After the final sanding is completed, the floor will feel smooth, but it won't quite be ready to receive the varnish. Additional smoothing is required, only this time use an electric buffing machine fitted with a sanding

SAFETY FIRST

When applying varnish, open the windows in the room for ventilation and wear a dual-cartridge respirator —not a dust mask—as protection against the noxious fumes.

4. Spread on a second varnish coat using the lamb's wool applicator. Let the finish dry overnight, then smooth the floor with a 220-grit sanding screen. Vacuum the floor clean.

5. Apply a third and final coat of varnish, and then let the surface dry overnight.

6. Install baseboard and shoe molding around the room perimeter, making sure to nail the moldings to the wall studs, not the flooring.

ENGINEERED-WOOD PLANKS

When it comes to do-it-yourself hardwood flooring, it's hard to beat engineered-wood planks. The flooring comes in long, wide tongue-and-groove planks that snap together and "float" over a thin foam underlayment; it's not nailed or glued down in any manner. And the planks come prefinished, so there's no sanding, staining, or finishing required.

Engineered-wood flooring was introduced to North America in 1984 by Kährs International, a Swedish flooring manufacturer. Today there are several companies offering this popular, easy-to-install flooring. Each engineered plank is composed of laminated wood layers, not unlike plywood, topped with hardwood strips. And because hardwood is used only for the top layer, engineered wood is available in many more wood species than traditional solid-hardwood flooring. For example, Kährs offers flooring in more than 20 wood species, including many exotics. In the master bedroom shown here, I installed Kährs Red Oak Sierra wide-plank flooring over a plywood subfloor. ▶ ▶ ▶

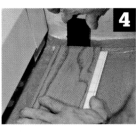

Tools and Materials

You'll need a few carpentry hand tools to install a floating engineered-wood floor, including a hammer, chisel, and layout square. You'll also need a saw to crosscut the planks to length and to rip them to width. You could make all the cuts with a handsaw, but that would be rather time-consuming. Alternatively, you could use either a circular saw or jigsaw for all cuts. I prefer to use both power saws. To rip planks for the first and last rows, I set up sawhorses outdoors and use a circular saw. But I make all the cross-cuts indoors with a jigsaw, placing the planks over a bucket to catch the dust.

There's one specialty tool that you'll need: a pull bar, which you can find at flooring dealers. The pull bar is used to snug up the planks in the last couple of rows and other places where there's not enough room to swing a hammer.

Engineered-wood flooring comes packaged in tightly wrapped plastic bundles. It's important to leave the bundles intact—don't cut them open—and stack them inside for a few days to acclimate them to the room's air temperature and humidity.

Left to right from the top: T-square, jigsaw, circular saw, pneumatic nailer, kneepads, utility knife, layout square, hammer and 2×4 tapping block, several ½-in.-thick spacers, pull bar, and wood chisel.

Engineered wood should be stacked indoors in unopened bundles.

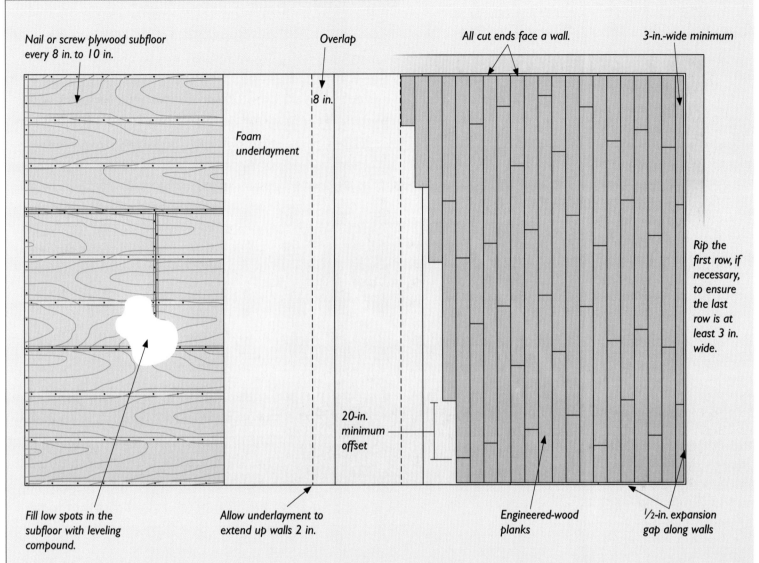

Nail or screw plywood subfloor every 8 in. to 10 in.

Overlap

All cut ends face a wall.

3-in.-wide minimum

8 in.

Foam underlayment

Rip the first row, if necessary, to ensure the last row is at least 3 in. wide.

20-in. minimum offset

Fill low spots in the subfloor with leveling compound.

Allow underlayment to extend up walls 2 in.

Engineered-wood planks

1/2-in. expansion gap along walls

Ready the Room

The first step is to empty the room of all furniture. If that's not practical, pile up all the furniture on one side of the room, remove the old floor from the other half of the room, lay some new flooring, then move all the furniture onto the newly installed flooring. This technique is suitable for large spaces, but for average-size rooms, say those less than 144 sq. ft., you're better off just emptying the entire room.

Engineered-wood flooring can be installed over virtually any sound, hard, flat surface, including existing vinyl, wood, laminate flooring, or even concrete or ceramic tile. However, it's always preferred to lay the planks over a clean, stable subfloor. For this installation, we removed old carpeting and then prepared the subfloor for the foam underlayment.

1. Pull up wall-to-wall carpeting by hand, starting in the corner. Use a utility knife to cut the carpeting into manageable pieces, so it'll be easier to carry the carpet from the room.

2. Remove the wooden tack strip from around the perimeter of the room using a hammer and pry bar, as shown in **A**. The strips are studded with hundreds of very sharp tacks, so handle them carefully.

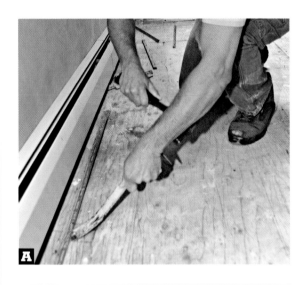

A

B

3. After removing all the tack strips, sweep a gloved hand across the subfloor feeling for nails that may have pulled through the tack strips. Pry up any nails that you find.

4. Now, securely fasten the plywood subfloor to the floor joists to eliminate any soft, spongy spots or annoying squeaks. The quickest, easiest way to secure the plywood is with a pneumatic nailer, as shown in **B**. However, you could also use a hammer and nails or a drill/driver and drywall screws.

Sweep the subfloor clean of all debris, then vacuum the surface to remove any remaining dust and grit.

Install the Underlayment

Engineered-wood flooring is installed over a thin foam-rubber underlayment that's simply rolled out across the floor. The underlayment plays an important role: It provides a cushioning layer, acts as a moisture barrier, and helps level out any unevenness in the subfloor. There are a few different types of underlayment available, but it's important to use one recommended by the flooring manufacturer. Failure to do so could void the flooring's warranty.

The 40-in.-wide underlayment, like the flooring itself, isn't fastened down to the sub-floor. It simply sits directly on the plywood. You could cover the entire subfloor with underlayment and then begin installing the floor planks. But I prefer to roll out two widths of underlayment, lay some flooring, then roll out more underlayment. That way, you reduce the risk of ripping or damaging the underlayment during the installation of the planks.

1. Starting against one wall, roll the underlayment across the room, as shown in **A**. Be careful not to rip the underlayment with the toes of your shoes. Smooth any wrinkles with your hands.

2. Cut the underlayment about 4 in. longer than the room width using a T-square and sharp utility knife, as shown in **B**. If you don't own a T-square, align a framing square with the edge of the underlayment, then place a straight 4-ft.-long 1×4 against the square. Run the knife along the edge of the 1×4 to make a square cut.

3. Set the cut piece of underlayment into position with its ends extending about 2 in. up the walls, as shown in **C**. The upturned underlayment will help shield the ends of the flooring from moisture.

4. With the first length of underlayment in position, roll out a second piece, cut it to size, and then lay it alongside the first piece. Lift the edge of the second underlayment piece and unfurl the plastic overlap flap to reveal the self-stick adhesive strip. Peel off the protective paper from the adhesive strip, as shown in **D**.

5. Lay the overlap flap on top of the first piece of underlayment, then press down along the adhesive strip to adhere the two pieces together, as shown in **E**. When sealing two pieces of underlayment together, be sure that only the plastic flap overlaps the first piece. The ⅛-in.-thick foam layer of the underlayment pieces should butt together, not overlap, creating a smooth, even surface.

To ensure good adhesion between sheets of underlayment, take a barely dampened cloth and wipe any dust and dirt from the surface of the previously installed underlayment. Then, peel off the protective strip from the next sheet of underlayment and stick it down.

Start Flooring

As with most types of plank flooring, a successful engineered-wood installation relies heavily on how well you install the first couple of rows. Begin by measuring the width of the room to determine whether or not you need to rip down the planks in the first row. If you skip this initial calculation and simply start with full-width planks, you may end up with a narrow sliver of flooring along the far wall. It looks best if the first and last rows are approximately the same width, but it's far more important that neither row be less than 3 in. wide.

To calculate the width of the first and last rows, subtract 1 in. of expansion space from the room width, then divide by 5⅛ in. (the width of each plank). That'll give you the number of full-width planks needed to cover the floor, plus the width of any remaining board. If the remaining board is less than 3 in. wide, you must cut down the planks in the first row the appropriate amount so that the last row is at least 3 in. wide.

For our installation, we had to rip about 1½ in. off the first row to ensure the planks in the last row were wide enough.

Install the first row

As mentioned earlier, to limit the amount of dust created in the room where you're working, make all rip cuts outdoors with a circular saw. Crosscutting with a jigsaw produces much less dust, so you can make those cuts in the room.

1. If you need to rip the planks in the first row, turn them upside down and make the cuts, as shown in **A**. For this particular flooring, the first row is installed with the tongue edge facing the wall and the groove edge facing out into the room. Therefore, the tongue edge was cut off when the planks were ripped down to size. Be sure to read the installation instructions for your flooring to ensure you're trimming off the correct edge.

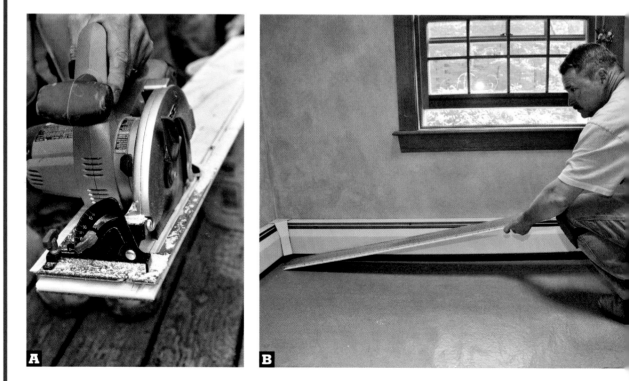

C

D

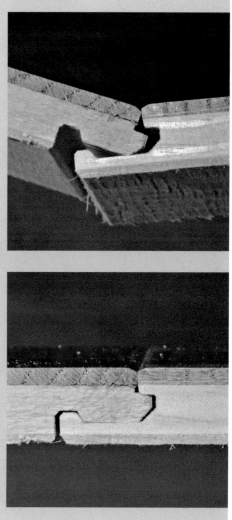

E

2. Set the first plank into position along the starting wall, as shown in **B**. Keep the plank end ½ in. away from the sidewall.

3. Take another full-length plank and butt it against the end of the first plank. Hold the second plank at an approximate 45-degree angle, as shown in **C**. Push the planks together, then lower the second plank flat to the floor. You'll hear the end joint click together. Continue installing full-length planks across the starter wall.

4. Cut the last plank in the first row to length using a jigsaw, as shown in **D**. Be sure to allow for ½ in. of expansion space at the sidewall.

5. Install the last plank in the first row, then slip a ½-in.-thick spacer block between the plank and wall, as shown in **E**.

Click-Lock Flooring

THE FIRST GENERATION OF engineered-wood flooring had traditional tongue-and-groove joints that had to be glued along every seam and joint. Although there are still some glue-together products, most modern engineered-wood floors have glueless, snap-together planks.

The Kährs floor installed here features the company's Woodloc system. Each plank is milled with a modified tongue-and-groove joint that snaps together with surprisingly little effort. The tongue edge has a locking groove milled along the bottom of the plank. The groove edge has an extended lower lip with a raised ridge that fits into the locking groove of the mating plank.

To assemble the floor, tilt the plank at approximately 45 degrees, insert the tongue into the groove, then lower the plank until the joint locks together. A slight tap with a hammer and tapping block will snug up the seam.

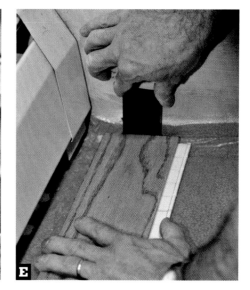

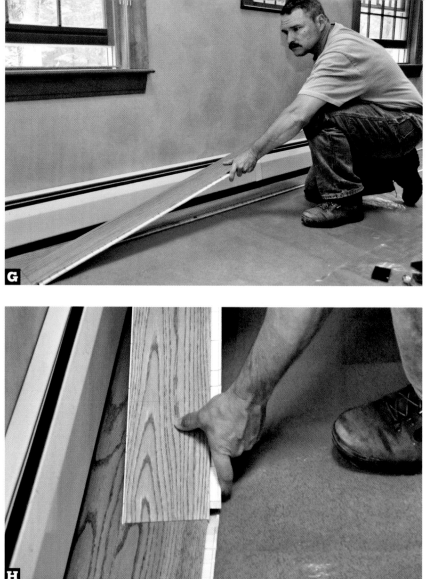

WHAT CAN GO WRONG

When using a tapping block to tighten up seams between planks, be sure to hold the block against the protruding lip of the plank's grooved edge. If the block comes in contact with the hardwood layer, it might chip off the factory-applied finish.

Lay the second row

Cut the first plank in the second row at least 20 in. shorter than the first plank in the first row to create the proper end-joint stagger. And be sure to cut off the tongue end of the plank, leaving the groove end intact.

1. Hold the first plank in the second row at about 45 degrees and press it into the first row, as shown in **F**. Push down to lock the joint together. If necessary, use a hammer and 2×4 tapping block to lightly tap the joint fully closed.

2. Hold a full-length plank at an angle and push its groove end against the tongue end of the previously installed plank, as shown in **G**. Lay the plank flat against the floor, then raise the long outside edge of the plank and tap it slightly to engage the edge joint.

3. Cut the last plank in the second row to length. However, this time cut off the groove end and keep the tongue end. Hold the plank at a 45-degree angle and press it down into place, as shown in **H**.

Install a third row of planks, using the methods described already. Then set several ½-in.-thick spacer blocks along the starter wall and push all three rows tight against the blocks. Also install spacers along the sidewalls to maintain the ½-in. expansion space.

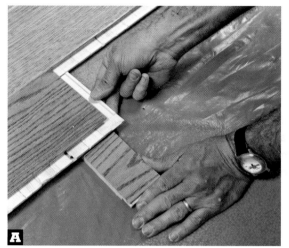

Continue Flooring

Continue to work your way across the room, making sure to leave a ½-in. expansion space along the walls, and to stagger all end joints by at least 20 in. from the seams in the previous row.

Installing floor planks is a repetitive process, so you'll eventually develop a working rhythm and discover a few techniques or tools that'll make the job go more smoothly. During this installation I found that using a small scrap of flooring as a shim made it much easier and faster to snap the planks together.

The tongue-and-groove joints milled into the planks will snap together easily, but only if they're properly aligned. If the two planks are off by just a little, you won't be able to snug up the joint.

1. Before trying to join one plank to another, take a small cutoff piece of flooring and slip it under the edge of the last installed plank, as shown in **A**. Position the scrap block within an inch or so of the plank end.

2. Install the next plank, starting with the end joint. Raise the plank to approximately 45 degrees and press it tightly into the end of the last installed plank, as shown in **B**. Lower the plank down until the end joint snaps closed. If it doesn't, raise the plank and try again.

3. Set a 2×4 against the edge of the plank and lightly tap it with a hammer to close the joint, as shown in **C**. Pull out the scrap block, slip it under the far end of the just-installed plank, and repeat the process.

Looking for Trouble: Glue Globs

THE PRECISELY MILLED JOINTS IN the flooring planks create incredibly tight seams, but even the very smallest obstruction will prevent the joints from fully closing. If you have trouble joining together two planks, especially at end seams, look closely where the top hardwood layer is adhered to the middle lamination. Occasionally you'll find a small, hardened glob of glue that squeezed out during the manufacturing process. Use a utility knife to carefully trim away the glue, being careful not to damage the hardwood layer.

4. As you make your way across the room, plank by plank, it's important to follow the same sequence, including joining the planks together starting with the end joints, as shown in **D**.

5. When you progress to within 12 in. or so of the edge of the underlayment, stop and install another sheet of underlayment, as shown in **E**.

Work around Doorways

Eventually you'll need to cut the flooring to fit around doorways. But rather than notching the planks to accommodate the door trim, it's much easier to cut the casings and jambs and slip the flooring underneath. However, that means you won't be able to tilt the planks to 45 degrees and snap them into place; they must be laid down flat and slid into position, as shown in the following section.

1. Start by laying a floor plank upside down in front of the door casing. (In that position, you won't scratch up the finished surface.) Next, hold a handsaw flat against the plank and saw through the casing, as shown in **A**. Repeat to trim the remaining door casings and jambs.

2. Cut the flooring planks to fit around the doorway, notching them if necessary, but making sure to leave a ½-in. expansion space. Then use a chisel to shave off the small ridge running along the extended lower lip of the plank, as shown in **B**. That'll allow you to slide the plank into place without tilting it up.

Note that depending on whether the flooring runs parallel with or perpendicular to the doorway, you may need to alter more than one plank. You may also need to use a pull bar and hammer to install the planks.

3. With the lower lip of the plank chiseled smooth, apply a bead of glue along the lip, as shown in **C**. To ensure a long-lasting bond, it's important to apply a continuous bead of glue along the entire lip of the plank.

Now slide the plank underneath the door casings and use a hammer and 2×4 block to tap it tight against the adjacent plank.

Finishing Steps

Installing the last row of flooring presents the same challenges as working around doorways: You can't tilt up the planks to snap them into place. Fortunately the solution is basically the same: Chisel the lower lip smooth and glue the planks together. Remember that you must chisel smooth the lower lip on the planks in the next-to-last row and rip off the groove edge from the planks in the last row, keeping the tongue edge intact.

A

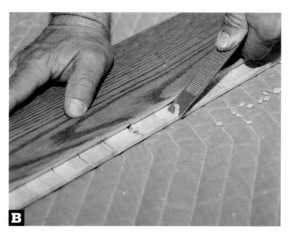
B

C

TRADE SECRET

An easy way to install the last row of flooring is to first snap together all the planks end-to-end, essentially creating one long plank. Then, slide the assemblage into place and draw it closed with a hammer and pull bar.

Install the last row

1. Once the next-to-last row of planks is installed, take a measurement to determine the width of the planks in the last row, as shown in **A**. Be sure to subtract ½ in. for the expansion space.

2. After chiseling off the ridge from the lower lip on the next-to-last row, apply a continuous bead of glue along the lip, as shown in **B**.

3. Rip the last row of planks to the proper width, keeping the tongue edge intact. Slip the planks into position, then use a hammer and pull bar to tap the planks into place, as shown in **C**. Slide the pull bar down a few inches and repeat along the entire length of each plank.

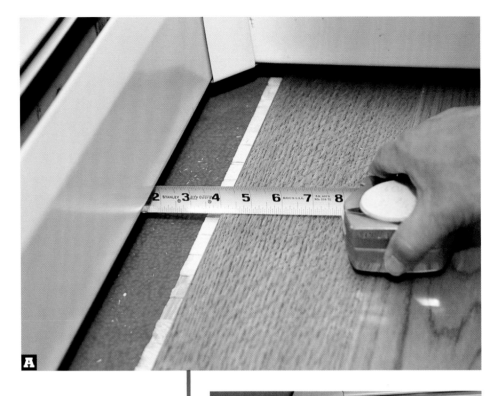

A

B

C

Add trim

1. Remove all the spacer blocks from around the room perimeter. Then use a sharp utility knife to trim the excess underlayment flush with the surface of the floor, as shown in 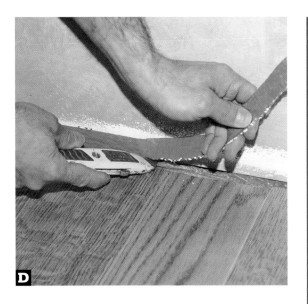.

2. Install baseboard on top of the flooring, as shown in **E**. Shoe molding can then be added, as well, if desired. Be sure to nail the moldings to the wall—not the floor—so the flooring can expand and contract freely.

D

Before installing base-board trim, mark the locations of the wall studs onto the floor or wall with painter's tape. Then you'll be sure to nail the molding to the studs, not just drywall.

E

TRADITIONAL PINE-PLANK FLOORING

There are many types of hardwood flooring you can install yourself, such as the hardwood strip and engineered planks shown on pp. 20–33 and pp. 34–47. Both are beautiful and extremely durable, but there's a softwood alternative to consider as well: No. 2 pine boards that are commonly available at lumberyards and home centers. Not only are these 1×10 boards easy to find and affordable, but they're also simple to install. They can be cut, laid, and sanded with standard carpentry tools, and the dust they produce isn't as noxious as many hardwood species.

Being lightweight and workable makes softwood boards appealing to install but also prone to damage. Dropped cans, sliding furniture, and knocked-over tables, to say nothing of high-heeled shoes, can easily scratch and dent the surface. But none of this damage hurts the floor structurally and most of it can easily be repaired. Besides, most people think a little wear and tear lends character to a traditional pine-plank floor, especially when it's installed in an older house. ▶ ▶ ▶

Clockwise from top: jigsaw, cordless drill, ice scraper, comfortable kneepads, 4-ft. level, staple gun, a sharp handsaw, a chalk reel, a coping saw, layout square, utility knife and rosin paper, and a combination square.

Tools and Materials

Installing pine-plank flooring doesn't require much carpentry experience or many specialized tools. An assortment of common carpentry tools, like those shown here, should take care of the job nicely.

On this floor, we hand-nailed the pine boards to the plywood subfloor using masonry cut nails, which lends an Old World, handcrafted look to the finished floor. You could also use an air compressor and pneumatic nail gun to shoot the boards into place. That would certainly save time, but it wouldn't look nearly as nice.

Here are the tools and materials you'll need to install solid-pine boards:

- jigsaw for making cutouts around room corners, doorways, and other obstructions

- cordless drill for screwing down the subfloor and securing wedge boards for straightening a bowed pine board

- ice scraper to remove joint compound splatters and other dried debris from the subfloor

- comfortable kneepads

- 4-ft. level for use as a straightedge and for checking the subfloor for level

- staple gun for installing the red rosin paper

- sharp handsaw for cutting off the bottom of doorjambs

- chalk reel for establishing a straight starting line for the first board

- coping saw for cutting shoe molding

- layout square for making square cuts with a circular saw or jigsaw

- utility knife

- enough rosin paper to cover the floor

- combination square for marking straight layout lines

- 16-oz. to 22-oz. hammer

- several pounds of 2½-in. (8d) masonry cut nails

- nailset

- safety goggles

A big labor saver is a sliding compound miter saw. This powerful tool usually has an 8-in.- or 10-in.-dia. blade, and its motor slides on long support tubes. This type of saw is designed to cut on the push stroke, and most models have a crosscut capacity of about 12 in., meaning you can cut a 1×12 in a single pass.

Don't own a sliding compound miter saw? No problem. You can get by with a portable circular saw; just be sure to use a layout square to guide the saw for perfectly square cuts. If you're thinking of buying a power miter saw, be sure it can crosscut the width of the pine boards you're using before making the final purchase.

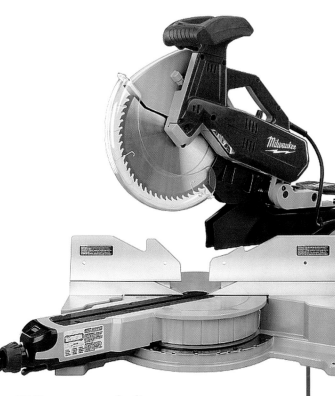

Sliding compound miter saw

And don't forget a wet/dry vacuum. You'll need it throughout the installation. From collecting dried joint-compound chips and general construction debris to sucking up fine sawdust, nothing cleans up a worksite faster and better than a good vacuum.

Site Preparation

If you are replacing existing flooring with new pine boards (instead of installing these boards in a new house) you have to remove the old flooring. Wall-to-wall carpeting is relatively easy to take out: Just pry off the shoe molding and start pulling up the carpeting at one corner. This will free it from the tack strip that holds it in place. Then work your way around the room, pulling up as you go until everything is loose. Roll it up, carry it out, and pry the tack strips off the floor. If the room has resilient vinyl flooring in place, you can install the pine boards directly over the surface. Just locate the joists using a stud sensor and mark their locations on the floor.

Cordless drills might be considered the default hole-drilling tool, but corded drills are more powerful and they never run out of juice at an inopportune time. Corded drills do need an extension cord, which is a nuisance on some jobs, but not when working on floors, and the extra power is always welcome.

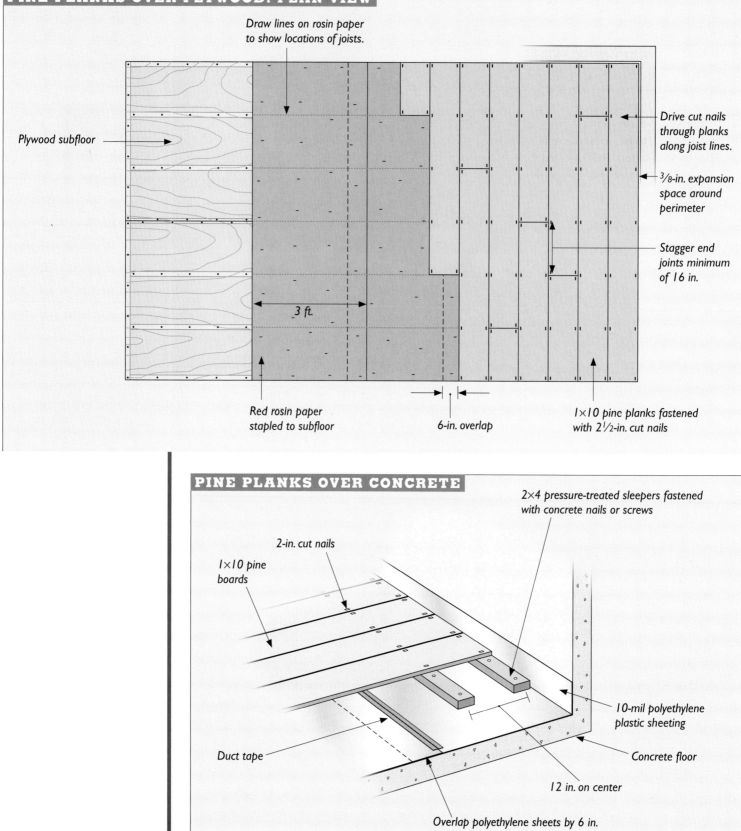

PINE PLANKS OVER PLYWOOD: PLAN VIEW

Draw lines on rosin paper to show locations of joists.

Plywood subfloor

Drive cut nails through planks along joist lines.

$^3/_8$-in. expansion space around perimeter

Stagger end joints minimum of 16 in.

3 ft.

Red rosin paper stapled to subfloor

6-in. overlap

1×10 pine planks fastened with 2$^1/_2$-in. cut nails

PINE PLANKS OVER CONCRETE

2×4 pressure-treated sleepers fastened with concrete nails or screws

2-in. cut nails

1×10 pine boards

10-mil polyethylene plastic sheeting

Concrete floor

Duct tape

12 in. on center

Overlap polyethylene sheets by 6 in.

Acclimating the Boards

ALMOST ALL, IF NOT ALL, PINE BOARDS sold at lumberyards and home centers are kiln dried, meaning their moisture content is between 8 and 14 percent. To stabilize the floorboards, it's a good idea to store the boards in the room where they're going to be installed for two weeks prior to installation. This will help reduce the chance of warping or twisting after the boards are installed. Stack the boards in the room with ¾-in.-sq. spacer strips—called stickers—between the courses. Don't cover the stacks of wood with a tarp, blanket, or anything else that will only trap moisture.

Remove the existing shoe molding and you're ready to go. Ceramic tiles must be removed, and solid hardwood flooring is generally easier and cheaper to refinish rather than cover with new flooring.

Once the old flooring is out, evaluate the existing floor. In most cases, this means simply checking for level and making sure the floor is reasonably flat, meaning no high points or low points of more than ¼ in. This is almost never a problem in new houses, but in older homes floors can settle significantly, especially if the joists are undersized. Low points, up to about ½ in., can be filled with floor-leveling compound.

A

Creating the right surface

It's easy to skip this first phase and just start nailing down the pine boards. But taking the time to properly clean the floor and prepare the room will save you time and trouble in the long run.

1. Begin typical surface preparation by removing any debris from the floor, especially dried joint-compound splatters and thick paint

drips. If there are just a few dried pads of compound, scrape them loose with a putty knife, then vacuum up the mess. But if the floor is covered with several dried pads, use a long-handled ice scraper, as shown in **A**. This tool makes the job much easier and faster.

2. Once the floor is scraped clean, walk over the entire length of each floor joist and listen for any squeaks. In new houses, the subfloor is usually tight to the joists, but in older houses

D

3. Check the clearance between the subfloor and the baseboards, as shown in **C**. If the space is greater than ¾ in., you can slide the pine planks under the baseboards. Just be sure to keep a ⅜-in. to ½-in. expansion space between the boards and the wall framing or drywall around the perimeter of the room. If the planks don't fit under the baseboards, maintain the expansion space between the flooring and the outside surface of the baseboards. If there are no baseboards, keep the floorboards ⅜ in. to ½ in. away from the drywall.

4. On the walls that are perpendicular to the direction of the floor joists, mark the position of the joists on the bottom of the drywall or baseboard, as shown in **D**. In most cases the position of the joists is obvious: You can see the nail heads securing the plywood subfloor to the joists. If the nail heads aren't visible, then use an electronic stud sensor to locate the joists.

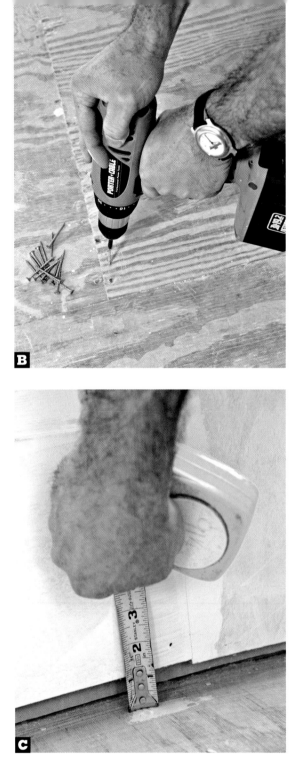

B

C

this isn't always true. Eliminating squeaks at this point is much easier than doing it later. When you hear a squeak, drive a 2-in. screw through the plywood subfloor and into the joist below, as shown in **B**. Drywall screws are the best fasteners to use because they are commonly available, cheaper than other screws, and are self-feeding so you don't have to drill pilot holes.

E

5. Doorjambs and door casings often rest on the subfloor because it makes installing the door easier. As a result, the doorjambs and casings often must be trimmed so the floorboards can slide underneath. The best way to do this is to put a scrap piece of flooring down in front of the jamb and place a handsaw on top to trim the jambs, as shown in **E**. The scrap piece of flooring serves as a cutting guide.

Installing rosin paper

This inexpensive paper is sometimes called "red building paper" or "slip sheet paper." It's traditionally been used between house siding and wall sheathing, and beneath wood flooring. With the advent of house-wrap products, the use of red rosin paper behind siding has nearly disappeared, but it's still widely used under flooring as a vapor barrier and a sound-deadening layer. It allows the floorboards to expand and contract over the subfloor without squeaking.

Rosin paper is typically sold in 3-ft.-wide rolls of various lengths. We bought a 167-ft.-long roll that has just over 500 sq. ft. of paper. If you plan for a 6-in. overlap between courses,

F

which is recommended, one of these rolls would cover about 415 sq. ft. of floor.

1. Get started by cutting the first piece of paper to length with a utility knife and spreading it across the floor. If you tuck it under the baseboard it'll be a little easier to control.

2. Staple the paper to the plywood subfloor using a staple gun filled with $\frac{3}{16}$-in.-long staples, as shown in **F**.

PRO TIP

Depending on where you're installing pine boards, you may need to cut off the bottom of existing doors so they can clear the flooring. The boards require $\frac{3}{4}$ in. of space. But you should also add some space for any rugs that may be used on the floors in the future. A carpet space of $\frac{1}{2}$ in. is generally considered adequate.

TRADE SECRET

After stapling down the rosin paper, sweep a gloved hand across the surface, feeling for any staples that aren't flush with the surface. If you find any offending staples, tap them down with a hammer. Raised staples can prevent the pine planks from laying flat and fitting tightly together.

3. Mark the joist locations across the top of the paper, using a thick marker and a 4-ft. level, as shown in **G**. Align the level with the joist marks you made earlier on the baseboard, and with the nail heads that are visible on the section of subfloor that isn't covered with paper.

You can cover the entire floor with rosin paper at this point, but it's easier to roll out one piece of paper, lay some pine planks, then roll out another length of paper. That way you won't damage the rosin paper by walking across it repeatedly.

4. To establish a straight line for the first board, snap a chalkline onto the paper about 9⅝ in. from the wall, as shown in **H**. (That's 9¼ in. for the width of a 1×10 pine board, plus ⅜ in. for the expansion space.)

In our case, starting the floor with a full board meant that we would have a full board to finish the room, including the closet door opening. Be sure to check the width of the first and last row of floorboards before nailing them in place. You don't want to start with a full board and end up with a sliver of flooring against the opposite wall. Pine-plank flooring looks best when the first and last boards are each about half the width of a full board. If necessary, rip the first board narrower to make the last board wider.

To determine the width of the last board, measure the width of the room and divide by 9.25 (the width of each 1×10 floorboard). That'll give you the number of full-width boards needed to cover the floor, plus the width of any remaining board. If the remaining board is less than half the width of a full board, rip the first board down to the appropriate width so the last board is about 4 in. to 5 in. wide.

Inspecting the boards

Installing pine-plank flooring would be much easier if all the boards were perfectly straight and flat, but unfortunately they aren't. Here's how to deal with less-than-perfect boards: First inspect them, as shown here, and set aside boards that are badly deformed. Stock that is bowed more than ½ in. over 16 ft. shouldn't be used for flooring. The same is true for boards that have a cup greater than ¼ in. across the width.

Save boards that are moderately bowed—more than ¼ in., but less than ½ in. over 16 ft.—and cut them into shorter, straight pieces.

1. Checking for a cup is easy. Just sight across the width of the board and estimate how much the board is distorted from flat, as shown in **I**. If you want to get an exact measurement, at least for the first few boards, place the blade of a combination square or framing square against the board and measure the space between the blade and the deepest point of the cup. Most boards will be cupped a little, but avoid using any plank that's cupped greater than ¼ in.

When installing the boards, always put the concave side down and the cupped side facing up. Over time the cup will flatten out as traffic and furniture press it down. Occasionally a cupped board may split, but if the concave side is facing down, the split will occur on the bottom and it won't be visible from the top.

2. To check for bowing, sight down the board from one end. Hold the board flat and then on edge, as shown in **J**. A workable bow depends, in part, on the grain pattern in the individual board. Again, any board with a bow less than ½ in. over 16 ft. is acceptable.

I

J

Material Matters

PINE 1× BOARDS COME IN six standard—or nominal—sizes: 1×2s, 1×4s, 1×6s, 1×8s, 1×10s, and 1×12s. Listed below are their actual sizes.

Pine boards are popular for interior trim work and architectural features, such as bookcases and storage cabinets, because they're readily available and easy to machine, join, and install. Over the last 30 years or so, solid-pine boards have been substantially replaced by manufactured panel stock and synthetic trim boards. That said, all lumberyards and home centers carry a large supply of pine boards and will order what you need if it's not in stock.

There are usually a few different grades of pine available. The best grade, Clear, is free of knots and other blemishes. Clear stock is expensive and often must be special ordered. Also available are C-select and D-select pine.

The former is a slightly better grade than the latter, but both are high-quality products with just a few small, tight knots.

Common grades are much more, well, common, and are called by different names. No. 2 common features many knots, most of which are tight, and very few, if any, holes that pass through the entire board. This grade is sometimes called "premium common" to differentiate it from lesser stock used for rough construction. We installed No. 2 common 1×10s for the pine-plank floor shown in this chapter.

For some cabinetry jobs, the knots and color variation in common boards would be unappealing, but for a traditional floor these "shortcomings" are assets. They create variation and interest over large surfaces that would otherwise seem too plain.

Virtually any size board can be used for flooring, although

the wide-plank look is generally preferred—this means 1×8s, 1×10s, or 1×12s. Note that 1×8s and 1×10s are generally straighter than 1×12s, but the wider boards do go down faster and look better in larger rooms. Fasten 1×8s and 1×10s with two nails per joist, but use three nails per joist to secure 1×12s.

One shortcoming of pine-plank flooring is the lack of joinery milled along the edges and ends. Typically wood flooring locks together with tongue-and-groove joints. Pine boards are just butted together and face-nailed. Although this doesn't yield the tightest floor joints, it does create a rustic feel that is appropriate in restoration work (when trying to duplicate older construction practices) and in newer remodeling jobs (when a traditional appearance is preferred).

Nominal Sizes for No. 2 Pine Boards	Actual Sizes for No. 2 Pine Boards
1 × 2	¾ in. × 1½ in.
1 × 4	¾ in. × 3½ in.
1 × 6	¾ in. × 5½ in.
1 × 8	¾ in. × 7¼ in.
1 × 10	¾ in. × 9¼ in.
1 × 12	¾ in. × 11¼ in.

3. Once you've culled all the straightest planks, take a moment to check the stability of the knots that appear on the top surfaces. Usually a quick visual inspection will tell you if the knot is tight or loose, but it pays to lightly tap each knot with a hammer. If you hear a rattling sound, then the knot is loose. Loose knots can eventually lift up as the board dries out, catching on shoes, socks, and bare feet. Cut the boards to remove any loose knots.

Preparing the Boards

Before you can begin nailing down the pine boards, you must first prepare each plank to become flooring. During this prep stage you must crosscut one end of each board perfectly square. Then use a router fitted with a roundover bit to soften the long edges on the top surface of each plank. This slight rounding will prevent splinters.

Trim the boards to length

The quickest, most accurate way to crosscut the 1×10 planks is with a sliding compound miter saw, which cuts on the push stroke. When properly adjusted, they'll consistently make perfect 90-degree cuts.

If you don't have a sliding miter saw, you can get excellent results using a portable circular saw and layout square, which is often referred to as a Speed®Square. Start by marking the board to length and holding a circular saw so its blade aligns with the pencil mark. Slide the layout square against the saw shoe and make the cut by pushing the saw through the board while guiding it along the square at the same time, as shown in **A**. This technique takes a little practice, but after a few tries you'll be making perfectly square cuts.

Working Safely

ONE OF THE GREAT THINGS about installing solid-pine boards is the almost total absence of toxic materials on the job, at least before you get to the finishing process. The rosin paper doesn't outgas anything noxious, the nails are inert, and the boards release no more pollution than a fresh-cut Christmas tree. However, sawing the boards does create dust to which some people are allergic, so follow these five simple rules to protect yourself and everyone else in the house:

1. Close all doors that connect to the rest of the house. Staple polyethylene plastic sheeting over open doorways.

2. Open the windows and place an electric fan in one window; be sure it's blowing out.

3. Wear a dust mask or dual-cartridge respirator when cutting, routing, or sanding wood. Respirators provide better protection than dust masks, as long as you remember to replace the cartridge filters as recommended by the manufacturer.

4. Keep a powerful wet/dry vacuum nearby to clean up sawdust at the end of each workday. This will reduce the amount of dust tracked through the house and make the air inside the room easier to breathe.

5. Wear eye protection, especially when cutting, nailing, or sanding the boards. Most people prefer safety glasses, but safety goggles offer better protection because they completely cover your eyes.

A

TRADE
SECRET

Whenever possible

it's best to lay pine-plank flooring perpendicular to the floor joists. This way, you can drive the nails through the boards and into the joists below for maximum hold-down strength. If the boards run parallel with the joists, most of them would only be nailed to the plywood subfloor.

TRADE
SECRET

Small dents can

usually be fixed with nothing more than a hot, damp cloth. Soak a clean, cotton cloth in hot water. Squeeze out most of the water, press the cloth against the dent, and hold it there for a few minutes. The combination of moisture and heat will cause the softwood fibers to swell back to their original position. For severe dents, hold the tip of a hot steam iron against the damp cloth.

Rout the edges

1. After crosscutting each board, place a ⅛-in.-radius roundover bit into your router.

2. Set the router for a very shallow cut, then round over the top, long edges of each board, as shown in **B**. Rout just the two long edges, not the ends.

Note that you can also soften the edges with 120-grit sandpaper and a sanding block. Just wrap a one-quarter piece of standard sandpaper around a wood block. Sand the edges so they have a radius of approximately ⅛ in. The same job can be done with a block plane or wood rasp.

Laying the Boards

Before you start nailing the boards in place, make sure your shoes and kneepads are reasonably clean so you won't leave any indelible or damaging marks on the boards. When working with such light-colored, unfinished wood, any stain will most certainly need to be sanded out.

Installing the first row

1. Select a board that is straight and flat (or nearly flat) and lay it on the floor with its square-cut end about ⅜ in. from the wall. Mark the other end of the board at the center of a joist, then crosscut it to length.

Now lay the board on the floor with its outside edge on the chalkline, as shown in **A**. Make sure there's a ⅜-in.-wide expansion space along the walls.

2. Set the blade on a combination square to 1¼ in. and mark nail positions along the outside edge of the board so that each one lines up with the center of a joist, as shown in **B**. Locating all the nails in exactly the same position isn't required, but it does create a neat appearance for all fasteners that'll be visible for the life of the floor.

3. Once you've marked the outer nail positions, adjust the square to 8 in. and mark the nail positions near the inside edge (the one near the wall), as shown in **C**. Again, these nails don't have to be perfectly aligned, but the closer they are, the better the floor will look.

4. Position the first nail so that its broad, flat side is parallel with the grain of the wood, then drive it in place, as shown in **D**. Take care with your aim. Soft woods like pine can dent easily, especially when struck with a heavy steel hammer. To avoid damaging the boards, consider making a nailing shield, as shown on the facing page.

A

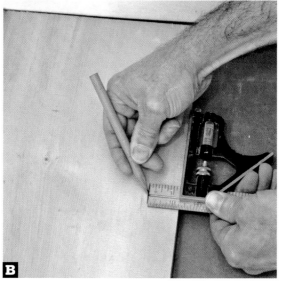

B

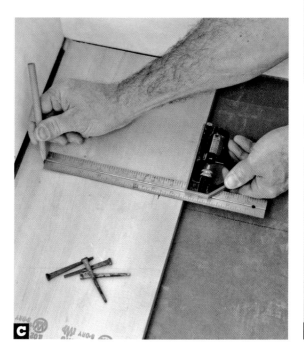

C

Nailing Shield: Board Protector and Thumb Saver

IT'S NO SECRET THAT PINE BOARDS DENT EASILY, especially when struck by an errant hammer blow. If just being careful were enough, then we could all just slow down and concentrate more. Here's a more realistic option: Fabricate a simple nailing shield, as shown here, from two pieces of scrap.

1. Take a piece of ⅛-in.-thick tempered hardboard (Masonite®) that's about 2 in. wide by 10 in. long and cut a 3⁄16-in.-wide by 3-in.-long slot into one end. I made the slot on a tablesaw, but you could also use a jigsaw, router, circular saw, or even a handsaw.

2. Make a simple handle from a ¾-in.-thick pine block that's about 2 in. wide by 3 in. long. Glue and clamp the handle to the hardboard, making sure the two pieces are flush at one end and that the rough side of the hardboard faces down. Allow the glue to dry overnight.

To use the nailing shield, first start the nail in the floorboard with a couple of light hammer taps. Slide the slot in the shield around the nail, then hammer the nail flush with the surface of the hardboard. Pull away the shield, and tap the nail head below the surface using a nailset and hammer.

A simple, homemade nailing shield prevents swing-and-a-miss hammer blows from dinging up the pine planks. The slot cut in the hardboard shield fits around the nail, effectively protecting the surrounding surface.

D

Fastening Options

I USED 8D CUT NAILS to attach these 1x10 pine planks to the subfloor. Like common nails, 8d cut nails are 2½ in. long, so they'll extend through the ¾-in.-thick planks and go about 1¾ in. into the subfloor and joists below. Cut nails hold much better than common nails because they're wedge shaped, which makes it very difficult for boards to pop loose. Cut nails are also very hard. However, because cut nails are so hard, they're also brittle and not nearly as malleable as common nails, making them much harder to pull out.

One of the great strengths of cut nails is that they have blunt ends, which push through wood fibers, instead of spreading them apart like the pointed tip of a common nail. As a result, cut nails reduce the chance of splitting a board. Still, it's a good idea to drill ³⁄₁₆-in.-dia. pilot holes when nailing within 2 in. of a board end.

Nailing isn't the only option for fastening pine planks. You could also screw them down with virtually any kind of screw. The only problem is that screw heads aren't very attractive. I suppose you could counterbore each screw and conceal it with a wood plug, but here's a better screw-down option: Fasten the boards with trim-head screws, which have tiny heads that you can drive below the surface where they'll become virtually undetectable.

Unlike a common nail (left), a cut nail (right) has a blunt tip and wedge-shaped shaft that provides superior hold-down strength. Be sure to wear protective eye goggles when driving any nail.

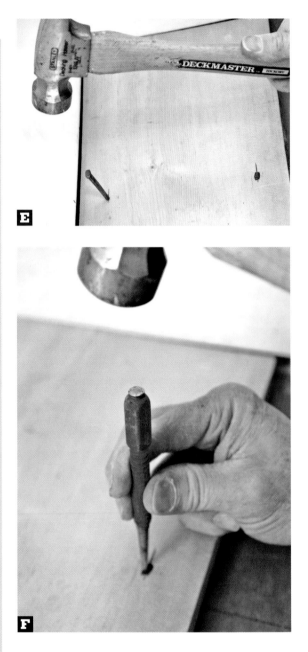

E

F

5. Drive another cut nail through the mark along the inside edge, as shown in **E**. Be especially careful to avoid striking the wall or base-board. If you do, the hammer will glance off course, causing you to miss the nail and strike the board.

6. After driving in a nail, use a nailset and hammer to tap the nail head below the board's surface, as shown in **F**. Setting nails takes some practice. You want to drive the head deep enough so it doesn't catch the abrasive paper when you sand the floor, or your toe when you're walking by. However, avoid overdriving the nail so that it creates a deep hole. The goal is to set the nail about ¹⁄₁₆ in. to ⅛ in. below the surface.

Nailset Options

THE JOB OF A NAILSET is pretty fundamental: Deliver enough force from a swinging hammer to drive a nail head below the wood's surface and—most important—to prevent the hammer from denting the board. This simple job is a bit complicated because there are different kinds of nails with different sizes and shapes of heads. For driving cut nails, however, there are two good nailset options: Use a traditional nailset with a ³⁄₃₂-in.-dia. tip, or use a Japanese-style nailset, which has a slightly broader tip.

The main difference between these two tools is that the traditional nailset is used in the vertical position, but the Japanese nailset can be used either vertically or horizontally. Using it horizontally not only keeps your fingers out of harm's way, but the tool's short, broad head is easier to hit and it delivers a more powerful blow.

Shown are a traditional nailset (far left) and a Japanese-style nailset (near left), which can be held either vertically or horizontally. Note that the traditional nailset has a non-slip rubber jacket that greatly dissipates vibrations.

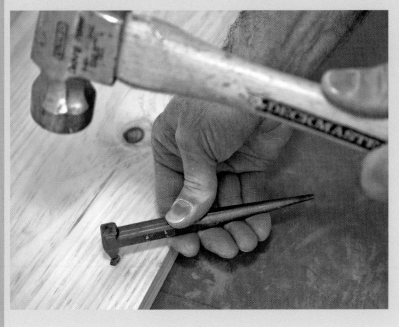

In the horizontal position, the Japanese nailset has a large head for easily tapping the nails below the surface.

PRO TIP

Before hammering in a cut nail, always check to ensure the nail's broad, flat side is parallel with the wood's grain. Otherwise, the nail will act like a wedge and split the plank.

WHAT CAN GO WRONG

When setting cut nails that were driven in at an angle, such as those securing the ends of the planks, be sure to hold the nailset at the same angle. Otherwise, when you hit the nailset with a hammer the nailset will slip off the nail head and damage the plank.

To ensure tight-fitting seams along the edges and ends of all the pine planks it's important to use a small broom to sweep away dust and debris from each and every joint. It only takes a small amount of dust to prevent two boards from fitting together.

G

Installing slightly bowed boards

1. Once the first board is nailed down, choose a board for the next row, cut it to length, and slide it in place, as shown in **G**. Be sure to stagger the end joints from one row to the next by at least 16 in.

Try to use the best boards to start and end the room with because they'll be the most visible. An area rug or furniture is often placed in the middle of the room. Bowed boards that must be cut in two should be used closer to the center of the room.

2. The best way to straighten a slightly bowed board is to use a pair of wedge blocks. Make the blocks out of 5/4 or 2×6 stock, as shown in the drawing below.

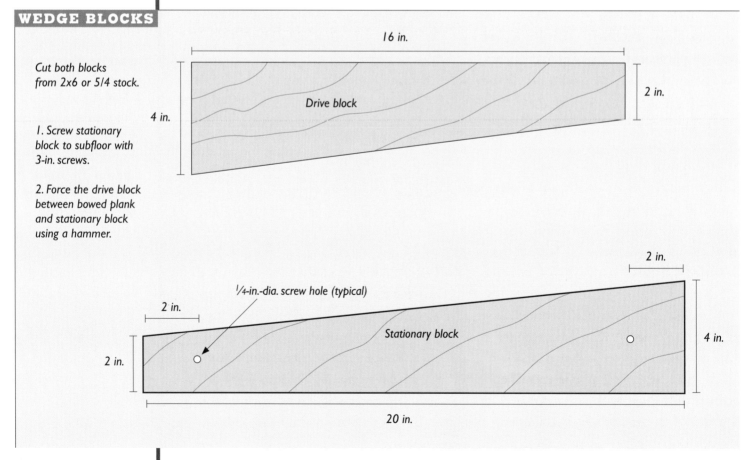

WEDGE BLOCKS

Cut both blocks from 2x6 or 5/4 stock.

1. Screw stationary block to subfloor with 3-in. screws.

2. Force the drive block between bowed plank and stationary block using a hammer.

16 in.

4 in.

Drive block

2 in.

1/4-in.-dia. screw hole (typical)

2 in.

2 in.

2 in.

Stationary block

4 in.

20 in.

To use the wedge blocks, set the longer stationary block on the floor with its angled edge facing the floorboard. Keep its straight edge parallel with and about 6 in. away from the floorboard. Screw down the block with 3-in. drywall screws, making sure the screws penetrate floor joists, as shown in **H**.

3. Once the stationary block is secured, slide the shorter drive block between the floorboard and the screwed-down stationary block. Tap the drive block with a hammer until the floorboard is forced tight against the adjacent board, as shown in **I**.

4. Now, with the wedge blocks securely holding the bowed floorboard in place, nail the board down to the joists, as shown in **J**.

Be sure to drive in at least four nails along each edge before removing the wedge blocks. Continue to use the wedge blocks, if necessary, to straighten out other sections of the board.

Making end joints

Unless you're installing pine flooring in a very small room, chances are you'll need to lay two or more boards to span from wall to wall. The first step is to make a good, square cut on the ends of the mating boards. A sliding miter saw is the ideal tool for this job, but as shown earlier, a circular saw and layout square can yield good results as well.

board can pinch the sawblade, spoiling the cut and possibly kicking the board back toward you.

1. Once the board is cut, test fit it to make sure that it falls directly over one of the joist lines marked on the rosin paper, as shown in **K**.

2. Mark the nail locations near the board's end, then bore pilot holes with a $\frac{3}{16}$-in.-dia. bit. Be certain to angle the holes slightly to ensure the nails will hit the joist, as shown in **L**. Brush away the wood chips so they don't fall beyond the end cut; a little debris can prevent the boards from fitting tightly together.

3. Put a cut nail into the pilot hole with its broad face parallel with the wood grain and drive it in at an angle, as shown in **M**. Leave the nail head protruding a little, then drive it below the surface with a nailset.

4. Once the first board is nailed in place, brush away any debris from the joint location. Then cut the mating board and slide it up against the first board, as shown in **N**. If both boards were cut squarely, they should butt together tightly. If

Whichever method you use, you'll need help holding long boards during cutting. You can set up various work supports, but a second pair of hands is the easiest and quickest solution. Have your helper hold the board level with the saw. If he raises it too high or pushes it down, the

they don't, make minor adjustments to the second board to create a tight fit. Gaps smaller than 1/16 in. are generally considered acceptable, but anything wider should be fixed by recutting the second board.

Continuing the flooring

1. Stop installing boards within 6 in. or so of the rosin paper edge. Then roll out a new course, overlapping the first by about 6 in., as shown in **O**. You can snap a chalkline to be sure the paper is straight, but just eyeballing the distance between the paper and the board's edge will suffice.

2. After stapling down the rosin paper, mark the joist locations using a 4-ft. level or other straightedge, as shown in **P**.

Continue installing pine planks and rosin paper in this fashion until you get close to the opposite wall. Laying floorboards takes some time and you may not finish in one day. Plan to protect the floorboards after working by closing off the room, or at least by covering the floorboards with a canvas or plastic drop cloth.

Flooring around Doorways

There are three basic approaches to installing flooring in doorway openings. When the planks are running straight toward a doorway, it makes sense to install a threshold across the opening and then simply butt the ends of the planks into the threshold. On the other side of the threshold you can continue the pine planks, or install some other flooring.

Plywood Inlay: A Flooring Shortcut

OFTENTIMES A WOOD FLOOR IS COVERED by an area rug that extends to within 3 ft. or 4 ft. of the walls. If you'll be putting down a rug, it doesn't make sense to cover the whole floor with pine planks. Consider this ingeniously simple shortcut.

Lay ¾-in.-thick plywood in the middle of the room and fill in around it with pine planks. This technique is less expensive and much faster than laying floorboards throughout. If you decide to take this shortcut, be sure to make the plywood section at least 2 ft. smaller than the rug. Here's how to create a plywood inlay (see the illustration below for more details):

1. Staple red rosin paper across the subfloor.
2. Snap chalklines onto the paper to represent the outline of the plywood section. When feasible, position the chalklines to run parallel with the floor joists so they fall in the middle of a joist.
3. Cut plywood to fit within the outline and fasten it to the subfloor with 2-in. drywall screws.
4. Cut and install the pine planks with 2½-in. cut nails, except where the planks abut the plywood inlay. There, fasten down the end of each plank with three 2-in. screws; that's necessary in order to pull the plank ends down flush with the plywood inlay.
5. Apply floor finish only to the planks; coat the plywood with primer or sealer, then top with a carpet pad, as recommended by the rug manufacturer.

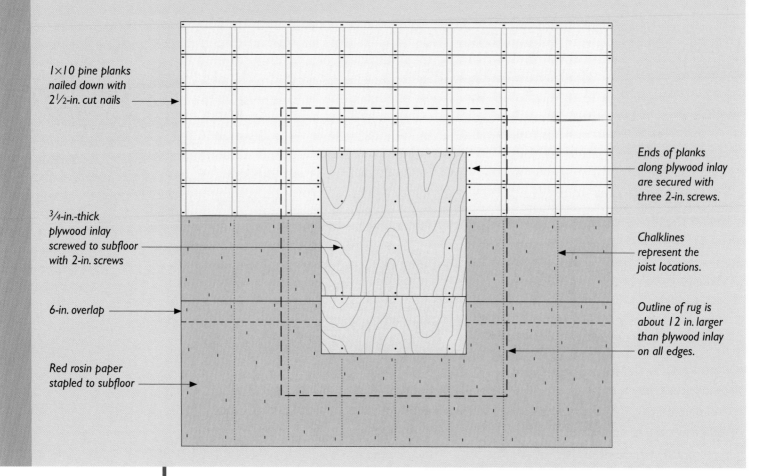

1×10 pine planks nailed down with 2½-in. cut nails

¾-in.-thick plywood inlay screwed to subfloor with 2-in. screws

6-in. overlap

Red rosin paper stapled to subfloor

Ends of planks along plywood inlay are secured with three 2-in. screws.

Chalklines represent the joist locations.

Outline of rug is about 12 in. larger than plywood inlay on all edges.

When the floorboards are running parallel to a doorway, you can continue laying planks right through the opening and into the space beyond. If you want the floorboards to end at the door-way, then just notch the last plank so that it extends across the opening, creating a threshold. Then you can install some other flooring in the space beyond the last pine plank.

Doorway thresholds

Thresholds are installed between the doorjambs and laid flat on the subfloor. But their width is not set in stone. Some carpenters cut thresholds to extend from the outside surface of the door casings on each side, a distance of about 5½ in. But a simpler approach is to cut the threshold to match the width of the doorjambs, which is what I did here.

1. Using the same pine stock as the floorboards, cut a threshold to fit snugly between the doorjambs and exactly the same width as the doorjambs. Test fit the threshold, and once you're satisfied, nail it in place using 2½-in. (8d) finishing nails.

2. Once the threshold is in place, continue installing the pine planks. Butt each plank against the threshold, as shown in **A**, and check for a tight fit. If necessary, recut the plank.

3. After nailing the first plank at the threshold, continue nailing down the rest of that board. Fasten another plank at the threshold and then nail it off along its length. Repeat in this manner until you've installed planks across the entire threshold. Continue installing planks across the subfloor as you did before.

4. If there's a door opening on the far wall and you plan to slide the last plank under the baseboard, you must stop two boards short of the wall. Then place a full-width plank on the floor and slide it tight against the last board nailed in place. Draw a line along the edge of this board and onto the rosin paper, as shown in **B**. This line serves as a reference point for marking and cutting the last board.

A

B

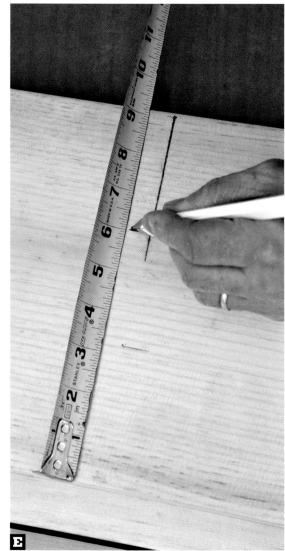

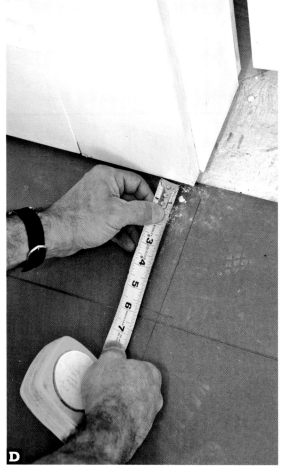

5. Slide this loose plank up against the wall and transfer the location of the doorjambs onto the plank using a combination square, as shown in **C**.

6. Remove the loose plank and measure the distance from the baseboard to the line drawn on the rosin paper, as shown in **D**.

7. Transfer the measured distance to the plank, as shown in **E**. Also measure between the baseboard and the line at a few other points, and transfer these measurements to the plank.

F

G

H

8. Use a straightedge to connect all the layout lines on the last board. If the plank is parallel with the last wall, you can draw a straight line using a combination square, as shown in **F**.

9. Notch the plank to fit around the doorway using a jigsaw, as shown in **G**. Don't worry if the cuts are a little rough, as they'll be hidden from view once the plank is installed.

Installing the last row

1. Once the last plank is cut to length and notched around the doorway, slide it into position, as shown in **H**. If the fit is too tight, don't force the plank. Instead, remove it and use the jigsaw to trim away some wood.

2. Use a hammer and scrapwood block to tap the plank into place, as shown in **I**. Align the outer edge of the plank with the layout line drawn on the rosin paper, but don't nail down the plank just yet.

3. Drop the next-to-last plank into place, as shown in **J**. If your layout lines were properly marked, this plank should fit easily between the last plank and the third-to-last plank.

4. Start a cut nail in the last plank. Then slip a pry bar between the plank and the baseboard or wall and push to close the gap between the last two planks, as shown in **K**. Keep pressure on the pry bar as you drive the nail into the subfloor. Then slide the pry bar down to the next joist location and repeat: Start a nail, pry the plank away from the wall, then drive the nail.

Installing Shoe Molding

Standard shoe molding measures $\frac{7}{16}$ in. wide by $\frac{11}{16}$ in. high and is installed around the room perimeter where the flooring meets the baseboard. However, you don't have to use shoe molding. Cove, quarter-round, and stop moldings can all be substituted, just be sure to use smaller versions of these profiles; $\frac{3}{4}$ in. or less are preferred.

On most jobs, the shoe is cut with a power miter saw and installed after the floor is finished. Here, we wanted to remove all the tools and equipment and vacuum up the dust and debris, so we precut the shoe molding and test-fitted the pieces without nailing them in place.

It's best to span the entire wall with one piece of molding. When that's not possible, join two lengths with a scarf joint by cutting each mating end to 45 degrees. Then overlap the ends to create a smooth, tight-fitting joint. The advantage to using scarf joints, instead of butt joints, is that if the molding shrinks a gap won't appear between the two mating ends.

Cut miter joints into the shoe at outside corners. At inside corners, use a coping saw, as shown in this section, to cut coped joints. Keep in mind that shoe molding should be attached to the baseboard, not the floor. This allows the floorboards to expand and contract without splitting. Use small 1½-in. (4d) finishing nails to attach shoe molding.

1. To cut a coped joint, start by making a square cut onto the end that fits into the room corner. If the shoe spans from wall to wall, cut

both ends square. If not, cut a scarf joint onto the opposite end. Push the shoe tight against the baseboard, then slide the square-cut end into the corner, as shown in **A**. If it won't stay in place, hold it temporarily with masking tape.

2. After installing the square-cut shoe molding, cut a 45-degree miter on the end of the mating piece of shoe, as shown in **B**.

PRO TIP

Before attempting to cut a coped joint with a coping saw, highlight the cutting line by rubbing the edge of the miter cut with a pencil. The darkened edge will be much easier to see as you guide the narrow sawblade through the cut.

TRADE SECRET

When driving a nail close to the end of a length of shoe molding, drill a pilot hole to prevent the 1½-in. finishing nail from splitting the molding. However, instead of using a small-diameter drill bit, chuck a finishing nail into the drill and use it to bore a perfect-size pilot hole.

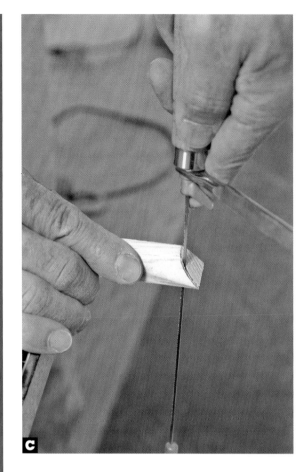

3. Use a coping saw to back-cut the end of the shoe, as shown in **C**. Carefully cut along the edge of the miter as you saw through the molding. Most people prefer to use a coping saw on the pull stroke instead of the push stroke, but the blade can be installed to cut in either direction.

4. Smooth the just-cut end of the coped joint using a round file or a piece of 120-grit sandpaper wrapped around a wood dowel. Then, slide the coped shoe into the corner and check its fit against the square-cut shoe, as shown in **D**. The joint should fit tight without any visible gaps.

If necessary, file or sand the coped end until it fits snugly. Continue cutting and fitting lengths of shoe molding around the room. When done, remove the moldings and paint them to match the baseboards, but don't install them until after the floor is finished.

Finishing Options

WHEN CHOOSING FLOOR-FINISHING products, first consider compatibility. This means buying the sealers, stains, and topcoats from the same manufacturer so you can rely on them working together properly. In broad terms, the biggest choice is between water-based (latex) products and oil-based finishes.

Years ago, high-quality water-based products weren't readily available, but these days you can find them at most lumberyards and home centers. They perform well, are a good alternative to oil-based products because they dry more quickly, give off less-harmful odors, and feature a clean, transparent appearance. Unfortunately, you do pay a slight premium for water-based products.

No matter which approach you choose, start with a wood conditioner. This stabilizes the wood fibers and makes the absorption rate the same across the entire floor. Pine, in particular, is notorious for looking blotchy after a finish is applied. Wood conditioner will even out the floor's appearance.

After the conditioner, you can apply a stain followed by three coats of polyurethane, or skip the stain and go right to the poly topcoats.

Equally as important as the finish is the proper preparation of the pine planks prior to finishing. This means renting an orbital floor sander, not a drum sander, which would be far too aggressive for the soft pine.

An orbital floor sander has a flat pad that vibrates in tiny circles. Different sizes of sanders are available, but one with a 12-in. by 18-in. pad is most popular. Various sandpaper grits are sold, though 80- and 100-grits are recommended for sanding pine.

Controlling one of these machines is much easier than a traditional drum sander. Just turn it on and slowly guide it back and forth across the floor. Don't sand in one spot for too long or you'll form a depression. But unlike a drum sander, you can move an orbital sander across the wood's grain without causing visible scratches.

Be sure to vacuum up all the dust before applying any finish. Then use the sander with very-fine abrasive paper (120- to 220-grit) to lightly sand between finish coats.

GLAZED-PORCELAIN TILE

There's no denying that installing a glazed-porcelain tile floor requires a significant investment of time, materials, and money, even in a relatively small room. But that's a small price to pay for the ultimate reward: A floor that's highly resistant to staining, virtually waterproof, easy to clean, and extremely durable. In fact, it's not unusual for a properly installed tile floor to last many decades with little or no maintenance.

In this chapter, I'll show setting 20-in. by 20-in. tiles over cement backerboard in a large, open kitchen. However, that was the easy part. First, we had to bust out the old ceramic tile, pry up a layer of ¼-in. plywood, and then refasten the subfloor to the joists by screwing right through an old vinyl sheet floor.

Most installations won't require this much prep work, but it goes to show that there are no shortcuts to a quality tile job. Also in this chapter, you'll see how to set tile directly over a plywood subfloor. ▶ ▶ ▶

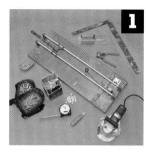

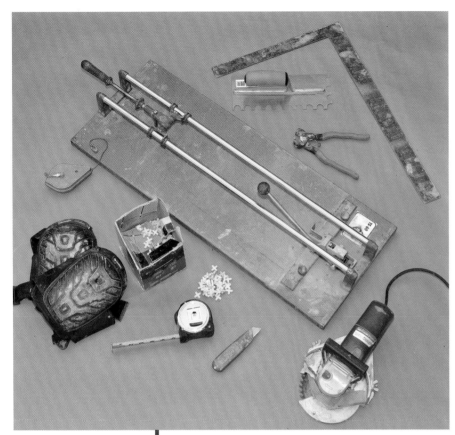

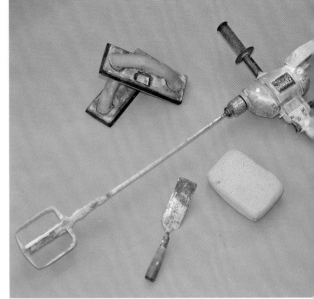

Other required tiling tools include (from top): rubber grout float, ½-in. electric drill and mixing paddle, margin trowel, and grout sponge. You'll also need a couple of plastic pails for mixing.

Standard floor tiling tools include the following (bottom from left to right): chalk reel, kneepads, tile spacers, tape measure, utility knife, and electric undercut jamb saw. Also needed are (upper right) a framing square, notched trowel, and tile nippers. Shown in the center is a manual tile cutter, sometimes referred to as a score-and-snap cutter.

Tools and Materials

The nice thing about laying a tile floor is that you need surprisingly few tools. Granted, most of them are specialized tiling tools, but they're all relatively affordable and easy to find at any well-stocked hardware store or home center. And the few expensive tools that you'll need, such as a tile cutter or wet saw, can be rented by the day. Even a ½-in. drill with mortar-mixing paddle can be found at most rental dealers.

For this particular job we also needed some demolition tools to rip up the old ceramic tile floor and the plywood underlayment beneath it. We used hammers and several pry bars of various lengths, but the bulk of the work was done with an electric chipping hammer, which we rented.

For a small room, one that's less than 30 sq. ft. or so, you could chop out the old tile with a hammer and stiff-blade putty knife or cold chisel. But for larger rooms, or for any tile mortared directly to a concrete slab, you absolutely must use an electric chipping hammer.

Tear Up the Old Tile Floor

Long before tiling can begin, it's important to prepare the existing floor for the installation of ¼-in.-thick cement backerboard. For this kitchen floor, we first had to strip off old ceramic tile and a layer of ¼-in. luaun plywood underlayment. Below the luaun we found vinyl flooring, which was in remarkably good shape, so we were able to lay the backerboard right on top.

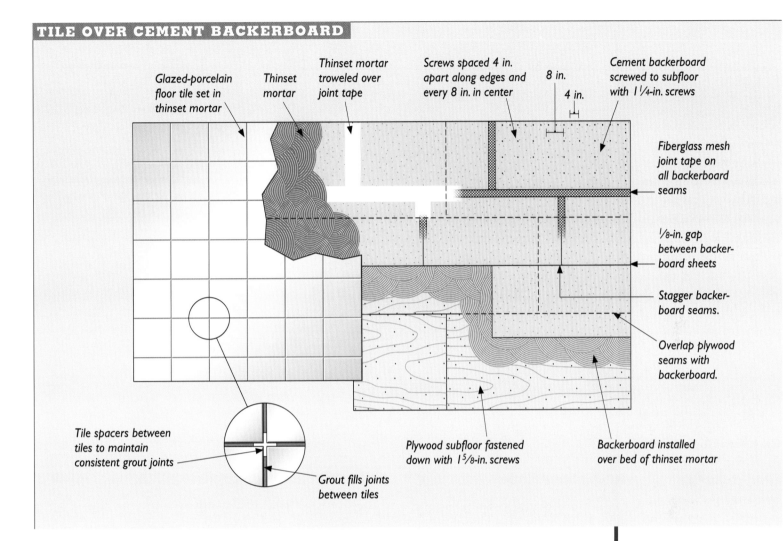

Glazed-porcelain floor tile set in thinset mortar

Thinset mortar

Thinset mortar troweled over joint tape

Screws spaced 4 in. apart along edges and every 8 in. in center

8 in.

4 in.

Cement backerboard screwed to subfloor with 1 1/4-in. screws

Fiberglass mesh joint tape on all backerboard seams

1/8-in. gap between backerboard sheets

Stagger backerboard seams.

Overlap plywood seams with backerboard.

Backerboard installed over bed of thinset mortar

Plywood subfloor fastened down with 1 5/8-in. screws

Tile spacers between tiles to maintain consistent grout joints

Grout fills joints between tiles

When doing any sort of demolition work, be sure to wear eye protection, work gloves, and a dust mask or respirator. And be aware that resilient (vinyl) flooring manufactured prior to 1986 may contain asbestos, a known carcinogen. If at all possible, leave the old floor undisturbed and cover it with plywood or cement backerboard. If it must be removed, hire an asbestos-abatement contractor. Never scrape, sand, cut, or tear out asbestos-laden flooring.

Start by removing any transition moldings or thresholds installed between the old tile floor and any other floors. Protect all adjoining floors from possible damage by covering them with thick blankets, moving pads, or 1/4-in. hardboard (Masonite). For this job, we removed the shoe molding, but left the baseboard molding intact.

Next, cover all doorways leading to the room with clear plastic drop cloths. This will keep dust from blowing all over the house but allow light to pass through. Tape the plastic in place, making sure it's long enough to extend across the floor by several inches. If necessary, weigh down the bottom of the plastic to prevent the wind from blowing it open. During the demolition process, it's also a good idea to place a box fan in an open window (blowing out) to keep the room clear of airborne dust.

When removing old ceramic tile, it's important to keep the chipping hammer at a low angle. To make this easier, hold the tool upside-down with its motor on top. That way you can get low to the tile without the motor hitting the floor.

WHAT CAN GO WRONG

After breaking up an old tile floor, carry the busted pieces from the room in a 5-gal. or smaller bucket. Tile is surprisingly heavy and a large box or trash can will prove too heavy to move.

A

B

The best place to start removing tile is at a doorway, where you can slip the chipping hammer's chisel bit under the edge of the tile. That's much more effective than beginning in the middle of the floor.

1. Place the chisel bit of the chipping hammer against the edge of the tile and squeeze the trigger, as shown in **A**. You don't have to apply much pressure, just hold the tool against the tile and the rapid-fire, percussive action of the chisel will shatter the tile into pieces. Continue to work your way toward the center of the floor one tile at a time.

SAFETY FIRST

When tearing out an old ceramic tile floor, be sure to wear safety goggles as protection from the sharp shards of broken tile.

Stop occasionally and clear the floor of the broken tiles. There's no fast, easy way to pick up the broken shards, but here's one method that works rather well: Use a heavy-duty dustpan to scoop up the pieces and dump them into a 5-gal. bucket.

2. If you must also remove a layer of plywood underlayment, force the chipping hammer's chisel under the edge of one sheet to partially loosen it. Then, use long wrecking bars to pry the plywood away from the floor. Once the plywood is sufficiently loose, force it up by hand, as shown in **B**.

As you work across the room, try whenever possible to pry up a sheet of underlayment without first chipping up the old tiles, as shown in **C**. That'll save time and quite a bit of clean up. Carry the large sheets from the room with the tiles still attached.

Busting Up Old Tile

AN ELECTRIC CHIPPING HAMMER provides the easiest way to remove old ceramic tile from a large room or long hallway. For smaller areas, however, you can get by with a hammer and stiff-blade putty knife. The manual method isn't nearly as fast, but it's less expensive and a whole lot quieter.

Hold the putty knife at a low angle against the edge of the tile and strike it with the hammer. Surprisingly, you don't have to pound on the knife to fracture the tile. Several sharp taps often work better than one he-man strike. If you don't have the proper putty knife, substitute a cold chisel or brickset.

Regardless of the tool or method you use, be sure to wear eye goggles as protection from flying shards of broken tile.

You can remove old ceramic tile with a hammer and putty knife—just be sure the putty knife has a steel-capped handle and thick, rigid blade. Hold the knife against the edge of the tile at a low angle so its blade gets under the tile but doesn't dig into the subfloor.

3. Before moving on to the next phase—installing cement backerboard—it's critical that the floor be free of any obstructions. Sweep a gloved hand across every square inch of the floor, feeling for protruding screw heads, nails, or staples left over from the underlayment. If you find any fasteners sticking up, there's no need to yank them out, just hammer them flush.

4. Once you've reached the bare subfloor or a stable layer of vinyl or linoleum flooring, sweep the floor clean of all large pieces of debris, then vacuum up the dust and smaller particles.

5. Slowly walk around the floor listening for squeaks and feeling for loose sections of subfloor. If you find any trouble spots, use a drill/driver to fasten down the subfloor with $1\frac{5}{8}$-in. drywall screws. You can place the screws anywhere along the floor, but for the best results, drive the screws through the subfloor and into the joists below.

Prepping the Floor

With the demolition work completed, it's time to prepare the subfloor by installing a layer of cement backerboard. Here, we used $\frac{1}{4}$-in.-thick backerboard, which is suitable for most installations. The 3-ft. by 5-ft. panels are lightweight, easy to cut, and relatively affordable.

You can also use $\frac{1}{2}$-in. backerboard, but be aware that the extra thickness can cause height problems at doorways, thresholds, and beneath undercountertop appliances, such as dishwashers

Tiling over Plywood: Good Idea or Bad?

THE PREFERRED METHOD OF tiling a floor is to set the tiles on top of cement backerboard, but that's not the only way to tile a floor. Long before the advent of backerboard, tile was laid directly over plywood. In fact, this method is routinely practiced today. And there's nothing wrong with setting tile over plywood, if certain conditions exist.

First, assuming the floor joists are spaced 16 in. on center, the plywood subfloor must be at least 1¼ in. thick. It could be one layer of ¾-in. plywood or oriented-strand board (OSB) topped with ½-in. plywood, or ¾-in. solid board sheath-ing covered with ½-in. plywood, or two ½-in. layers of plywood topped with ¼-in. plywood underlayment. Any combination that adds up to at least 1¼ in. is fine.

The problem is that many modern homes have subfloors comprised of two layers of ½-in. plywood, resulting in a 1-in.-thick subfloor that's not rigid enough to properly support a tile floor. So the bottom line is never set tile directly on a plywood subfloor that's not at least 1¼ in. thick. By the way, oriented-strand board isn't an acceptable substrate for tile, regardless of how thick the subfloor is.

A

Before spreading thinset mortar onto cement backerboard, wipe the surface with a damp sponge. That'll not only clean the surface prior to tiling, but it'll also slow down the porosity rate of the back-erboard so it doesn't immediately suck all the moisture out of the mortar, which could weaken the tile bond.

and trash compactors. The thicker panel is also much more difficult to cut.

Installing cement backerboard is necessary to create a stable, rock-solid surface for the tile. The reason most tile floors fail is because there's too much flex in the subfloor, resulting in broken or popped tiles and cracked grout.

However, to create a rigid, stable surface, it's imperative that you set the backerboard into a bed of thinset mortar. Too often I've seen jobs where the backerboard was screwed directly to the subfloor, and within a couple of years tiles started cracking and popping loose.

Spread the mortar

Thinset mortar is sold in 50-lb. bags at home centers and masonry suppliers. When possible, use the fortified type, which contains a powered polymer that makes the mortar stronger and more flexible. Just add water and mix. If you can only find regular, unfortified mortar, then pick up some liquid latex additive and mix that, not water, into the mortar. Note that thinset mortar is also used to set the tiles on top of the backerboard.

For one 50-lb. bag of fortified mortar, you'll need to add about 5½ qt. of water. However, it's best to mix up only about half of the bag at a time. Working in smaller batches requires mixing more often, but you'll be able to work at a more leisurely pace. Also, check the coverage rates printed on the mortar bag; you don't want to

mix up enough mortar to cover 60 sq. ft. if the floor is only 35 sq. ft.

1. Pour the water into a clean 5-gal. bucket, then add the mortar. If any hardened lumps of mortar fall into the bucket, fish them out, crush them into a powder, then add it back to the mix.

2. Use a ½-in. electric drill and a mixing paddle to blend the mortar and water mixture, as shown in **A**. Slowly raise and lower the paddle, making sure to press it all the way to the bottom of the bucket. Continue to mix the mortar for at least six to eight minutes until it's velvety smooth.

Once the mortar is well mixed, stop and let it slake, or rest, for at least five minutes. This time-out allows all the ingredients to coalesce. Then, mix it very briefly immediately before applying it.

3. Spread the thinset mortar across the floor using a ¼-in. by ⅜-in. notched steel trowel, as shown in **B**. Apply mortar across an area slightly larger than one 3-ft. by 5-ft. sheet of backerboard.

How Much Mortor Do I Need?

DETERMINING HOW MUCH THINSET MORTAR to buy depends not only on the square footage of the room, but also on the size of the notches in the trowel you're using to spread the mortar. For example, if you're using a ¼-in. by ¼-in. notched trowel, you'll be able to cover about 80 sq. ft. to 95 sq. ft. per 50-lb. bag of mortar. However, with a ¼-in. by ⅜-in. notched trowel, you'll only be able to cover 60 sq. ft. to 70 sq. ft.

Check with the tile manufacturer for the recommended trowel size, and then read the instructions on the thinset bag for approximate coverage rates.

Install cement backerboard

1. Lay a sheet of backerboard into the wet mortar, as shown in **C**. Shift the backerboard into position, if necessary, then press it down into the mortar by walking across the sheet.

2. Fasten the backerboard to the subfloor with 1¼-in. drywall screws, as shown in **D** on p. 84. We used an auto-feed screw gun, but you could also use a standard drill/driver or, better yet, an impact driver. Be sure to follow

SAFETY FIRST

Never use high-speed power tools such as a circular saw or grinder to cut cement backerboard indoors. These tools will generate excessive silica dust, which can irritate the lungs.

the screw pattern marked on the backerboard: Drive screws every 4 in. around the perimeter edges and space them 8 in. apart throughout the "field" or center of the sheet.

3. When necessary, trim the backerboard to fit the room using electric shears, as shown in **E**. You can also cut the sheets with a carbide-tipped scoring tool, but shears are much faster, cleaner, and more accurate. You can rent electric shears at most tool rental dealers.

4. Set the trimmed backerboard sheet beside the previously installed sheet, leaving a ⅛-in. gap in between. Then screw it down, as shown in **F**.

5. Use a damp cloth to wipe up any excess mortar that squeezes out from between the two sheets, as shown in **G**.

6. Continue spreading thinset mortar across the floor with a notched trowel. If the mortar in the bucket begins to stiffen up, discard it and mix up a fresh batch.

G

H

7. When necessary, use the shears to notch the backerboard to fit around wall corners and cabinets, as shown in **H**.

Tape the joints

Before tiling can begin, you must cover the seams between all the backerboard sheets with adhesive-backed fiberglass-mesh tape and mortar. As tempting as it may be, don't skip this step. Taping the joints is vitally important to create a continuous, monolithic substrate for setting the tile.

1. Vacuum the floor, making sure you remove any residual dust from the joints between the backerboard sheets. Next, unroll a length of $2\frac{3}{8}$-in.-wide fiberglass mesh tape, center it over a seam, and then press it down to ensure it sticks, as shown in **I**.

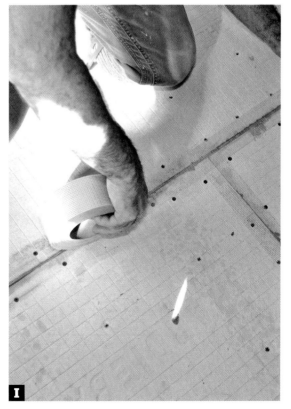

I

PRO**TIP**

Stagger all the joints in the cement backerboard. Never allow four corners of the sheets to meet at one point. And never align the edges of the backerboard with the seams in the plywood subfloor.

Two Tools for Cutting Casings and Jambs

IF YOU'RE TILING THE FLOOR of a room that has finished doorways, you'll need to trim the lower ends of the casings, and often the jambs, too, for the tile to fit beneath. That's much easier than trying to meticulously cut the tiles to fit around the doorways.

There are two basic ways to cut the door trim. The fastest way is with an electric jamb saw, which is a specially designed circular saw that you can find at most tool rental dealers. The saw has a horizontally aligned blade that you can adjust to the thickness of the tile.

The second way to trim casings and jambs is with a handsaw. You can use a standard carpenter's crosscut saw, but a Japanese-style pull saw works better. Its blade is thinner and more flexible, and it cuts on the pull stroke. When using a handsaw, it's necessary to place a tile down onto the subfloor or backerboard to position the saw at the correct height.

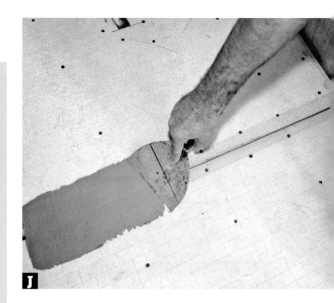

J

An electric jamb saw (top) provides the fastest way to trim door casings and jambs, but a handsaw (bottom) works just as well. Just be sure to first set down a tile for use as a height gauge.

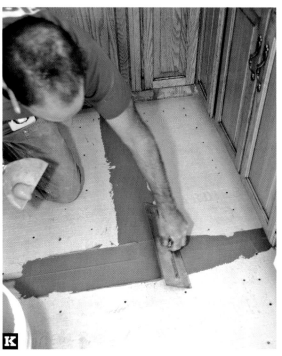

K

2. Use a 6-in.-wide drywall knife to spread thinset mortar over the taped joint, as shown in **J**.

3. Use a flat steel trowel (the kind without notches) to level the joint and remove excess mortar, as shown in **K**. The finished joint should be flat and smooth without any raised ridges or humps.

Setting Tile

For the kitchen shown here, we installed 20-in. by 20-in. glazed-porcelain floor tiles, which worked well in this large, open space. Tile this big, however, would be too large for the average-size room.

Generally speaking, small tiles, meaning those 12 in. by 12 in. or smaller, look best in small- to medium-size rooms. Larger tiles look best in bigger rooms. Fortunately floor tiles come in a wide range of sizes, colors, and patterns, so you're sure to find an appropriate one for your installation. And most manufacturers make the same color tile in many sizes, typically ranging from about 4 in. by 4 in. to 24 in. by 24 in.

The nice thing about working with large tiles is that you cover a lot of area very quickly. However, large tiles can't accommodate irregularities in the substrate nearly as well as smaller tiles can. If the substrate isn't extremely flat, large tiles tend to rest on high points or float over low spots. Both situations make the tiles susceptible to cracking. So, if the floor is a bit wavy or uneven, consider using smaller tiles that can better follow slight irregularities.

Before you start setting the tile, determine the best tile layout for the room. When the room is a simple square or rectangle, that's easy to do. Simply balance the tile pattern on the room center so that the cut tiles along the walls are the same size. However, laying out a balanced pattern is a bit trickier in a large, irregularly shaped room, such as this kitchen. We had to deal with inside and outside corners, four doorways, appliances, and cabinets. So we decided to balance the tile pattern off of the room's primary focal point: a pair of exterior French doors that serve as the kitchen's main entrance.

We started with a full tile at the French doors and ended with a 4-in.-wide cut tile at an interior doorway on the opposite side of the room. Not the ideal layout, but it was a reasonable compromise because it allowed us to also install full tiles in front of the cabinets on both sides of the U-shaped kitchen.

To ensure the first row of full-size tiles was perfectly straight, we snapped a chalkline onto the backerboard, making sure it was perfectly parallel with the French doors. We then used an undercut jamb saw to trim the bottom ends of all the doorjambs and casings, which is much easier than trying to notch the tile around the doors.

1. Start by mixing up a fresh batch of thinset mortar. Don't forget to allow the mortar to slake for five minutes or so before using it.

Spread mortar across the backerboard using a notched trowel, as shown in **A**. Apply the mortar along the chalkline, making sure you don't obscure the line. Work in sections no larger than about 15 sq. ft. That way, you won't have to rush in setting the tiles before the mortar begins to harden.

Always run tile under a dishwasher, trash compactor, and other undercounter appliance. Otherwise, you might not be able to lift the appliance over the tile when it comes time to replace or repair it.

PRO TIP

After setting cut tiles along a doorway, use a putty knife to force mortar under the edge of the tiles, filling all cracks and voids. That little bit of extra mortar will support the outer edge of the tiles and help prevent them from cracking or popping free.

Spread too much
thinset mortar at once and you'll have to rush to set the tiles before the mortar begins to harden. Play it smart and spread only 10 sq. ft. to 15 sq. ft. of mortar at a time.

TRADE SECRET

Mortar is somewhat
caustic and it can irritate your skin, causing painful rashes. Protect your hands by wearing latex gloves, or if you'd rather work gloveless, coat your hands in moisturizing lotion at the start of the day and each time after washing your hands.

B

For this particular tile, we applied the mortar with a rather large ¾-in. by ¾-in. notched trowel. Check with the tile manufacturer or tile salesperson for the correct-size trowel to use for your specific tile.

2. Set the first row of tiles into the mortar, as shown in **B**. Press down each tile with a slight twisting motion to ensure good contact with the mortar. Check to make sure the tile is aligned perfectly with the chalkline snapped on the backerboard.

3. Press the next tile into place beside the first one, then set a rubber spacer in the joint between the two tiles, as shown in **C**. The cross-shaped spacers are used to maintain even, consistent grout joints. The spacers are only temporary; you'll remove them later prior to grouting.

C

We used ³⁄₁₆-in. spacers on this installation because the large tiles require wide grout joints. However, smaller tiles generally have narrower grout joints, so they're set with smaller spacers. Check with the tile manufacturer for the recommended size spacer to use.

Once the spacers are installed, check the height of the tiles, making sure they're perfectly flush with each other.

4. Continue spreading mortar across the floor with the notched trowel. Again, work in relatively small sections, and if you come across any hardened lumps in the mortar, pick them out.

5. After applying the mortar, immediately drop a tile into place. Be sure you don't disturb or bump into any of the surrounding, previously set tiles.

6. Press the tile down into the wet mortar, as shown in **D**. Then carefully slide the tile into its final position, using spacers to maintain consistent joints between it and the adjacent tiles.

D

Mortar Test

WHEN SETTING floor tiles, it's a good idea to stop occasionally and check to make sure you're applying the correct amount of thinset mortar. Use a stiff-blade putty knife or margin trowel to pry up a just-laid tile and inspect the mortar on the underside of the tile. If the tile isn't fully coated, apply more mortar. Voids in the mortar will dramatically affect its bond strength and can cause the tile to eventually pop loose or crack.

Stop every now and then during tile setting and pry up a tile to make sure you're applying the proper amount of thinset mortar. The underside of the tile should be completely covered with mortar, with no voids or bare spots.

PROTIP

When using a notched trowel to spread thinset mortar, rake the mortar in straight, parallel lines, not in wavy swirls, which could trap air pockets beneath the tile.

E

F

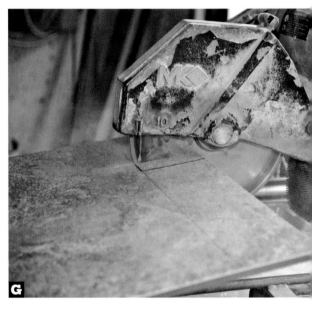

G

7. When necessary, trim a tile down to size with a manual score-and-snap tile cutter. Firmly press the tool's scoring wheel down onto the tile, then push it across the tile's surface, as shown in **E**. Next, set the tool's handle on top of the tile and press down to snap the tile along the scored line, as shown in **F**.

8. A score-and-snap tile cutter is ideal for making straight cuts, but when you've got to notch a tile you'll need to use a motorized wet saw. Set the tile onto the saw's sliding table, then push the tile into the spinning blade, as shown in **G**. Once you've cut as far as necessary, pull the table straight back away from the blade. Reposition the tile on the table, then slide it forward into the blade to make the second cut.

Four Tools for Cutting Tile

GLAZED PORCELAIN TILE IS extremely dense and strong, which makes it an ideal flooring material. But those characteristics also make it difficult to cut, unless you've got the right tools.

For straight cuts, use a manual score-and-snap cutter. The two-step process includes pressing the carbide wheel across the tile's surface to score the glazed surface, then pushing down on the handle to snap the tile in two.

When you need to cut a notch into a tile or make other precise cuts, use a motorized wet saw, which has a diamond-impregnated blade and a cooling water bath. The saw is equipped with a sliding table that allows you to safely and slowly push the tile into the spinning blade.

To make holes in the middle of a porcelain tile, use a drill fitted with a diamond-grit hole saw. Keep steady pressure on the drill, but don't press down too hard or you'll strain the drill

motor and slow the cutting process. If working with glazed-ceramic tiles, which have clay bodies, you can drill holes with a carbide-grit hole saw.

Tile pliers, called nippers, are used to "nip" away at tiles, removing one tiny piece at a time. Nippers are useful for fine tuning irregular cuts or trimming the edges of rough-cut tiles.

Manual score-and-snap cutter

Motorized wet saw

Drill and diamond-grit hole saw

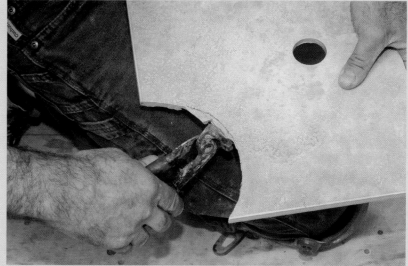
Nippers, or tile pliers

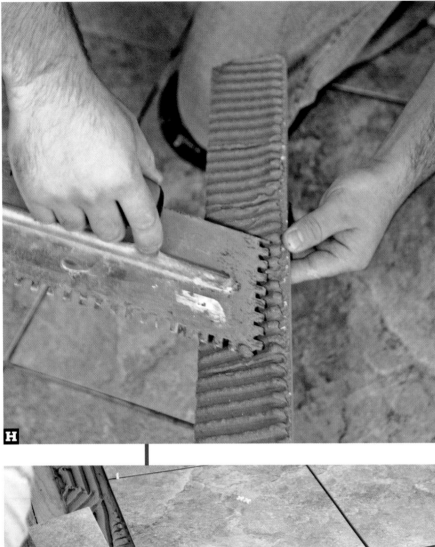

9. Trim the last row of tiles to fit, then spread mortar onto the backerboard with a notched trowel.

10. If the tiles are less than half the width of a full tile, also apply mortar to the back of the tiles (a technique known as back buttering), as shown in **H**. The double dose of mortar is recommended on small tile pieces to ensure a strong, long-lasting bond.

11. Set the last row of tiles into the mortar, making sure to use spacers to maintain even grout joints, as shown in **I**.

Once you've set the last tile, stay off the floor for at least eight to ten hours.

Grouting the Floor

Grout is used to fill the joints between the tiles. Like mortar, it comes in a powder that you must mix with water. Be sure to buy polymer-modified tile grout, which contains acrylic additives that make the grout much more water- and stain-resistant.

Grout comes in two basic types: sanded and nonsanded. Sanded grout is used to fill joints that are wider than 1/8 in.; we used sanded grout on this kitchen floor. Nonsanded grout, as you may have guessed, contains no sand. It's used to fill tile joints that are 1/8 in. wide or narrower.

Both types of grout are available in dozens of colors, so you won't have any trouble finding one to complement or contrast with the tile color. You can mix grout in a 5-gal. pail using an electric drill and mixing paddle, but that's not usually necessary because even large rooms require relatively little grout. That's why I prefer to mix small batches of grout in a 1-gal. or 2-gal. bucket using a margin trowel.

Spread the grout

The tool used to force grout into the tile joints is called a rubber float. It's basically a trowel faced with a thick, dense slab of rubber.

1. Start by removing all the rubber spacers from between the tiles. If necessary, use a putty knife or slotted screwdriver to dig out the spacers. Be careful not to chip or scratch the tile.

2. Scoop some grout out of the bucket with the margin trowel and plop it onto the floor. Then use the rubber float to force the grout into the joints between the tiles. Note that it's important to hold the float at an angle so you're both filling the joints and wiping off the excess grout at the same time, as shown in **A**.

3. Continue to work your way across the room, making sure to completely fill each tile joint with grout, as shown in **B**. Press down hard on the float and wipe it diagonally across

Using a Grout Color Chart

TILE GROUT IS AVAILABLE in more than 100 different colors, so picking the most desirable shade isn't always easy. Fortunately, most grout manufacturers have color charts that show each shade of grout offered.

When you purchase the tile, ask the salesperson for a grout color chart. Then, compare the grout samples against the tile's surface. Most installations look best when the grout closely matches or complements the color of the tile. However, there's no reason why you can't pick a contrasting color, which would highlight the tile pattern and the grout joints.

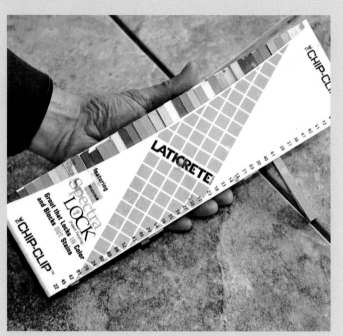

Picking a grout color is much easier with the help of a color chart. This particular chart has 40 slide-out color bars; each one represents a different grout color.

the tile joints. That'll help prevent the float from pulling any grout out of the joints.

Clean the tile

After grouting all the tile joints, you'll need to wait between 15 and 30 minutes for the grout to "set up" or partially harden before you can begin to clean the grout haze from the surface of the tile. Exactly how long you must wait depends on several factors, including the depth and width of the tile joints and the air temperature and humidity in the room. Grout will dry much faster on a hot, dry day, than on a cool, humid one.

The trick is to wait long enough that you'll be able to wipe the tiles clean without disturbing the grout joints. Wait too long, though, and the grout will dry on the tile, making cleanup much more difficult. To be safe, wait 15 minutes,

then do a small test: Take a damp sponge and clean the grout haze from one or two tiles. If the sponge wipes the grout from the joints, stop and wait another 10 minutes or so.

1. To clean the tiles on this job, we used a grouting machine, which is essentially a large, rectangular water bucket equipped with a set of squeegee rollers. Soak the sponge float that comes with the machine into the bucket, then press it across the rollers to squeeze out the excess water, as shown in **C**.

2. Hold the sponge float over the bucket and firmly wipe your hand down the sponge to remove the last little bit of water, as shown in **D**. It's important to use a damp—not wet—sponge because too much water will dilute and soften the grout.

Tiling Toe Kicks

TOE KICK SPACES BENEATH kitchen cabinets are usually faced with plywood that's finished to match the cabinets. In this kitchen we decided to replace the plywood with tile. This small upgrade not only creates a smooth, attractive transition from the new floor to the cabinets, it also creates a durable, easy-to-clean toe kick.

The cabinet toe kicks were faced with tile. Each narrow tile piece was back buttered with mortar, then pressed into place.

3. Hold the sponge float flat against the floor and use wide, sweeping motions to clean off the grout haze, as shown in **E**. Again, work the sponge diagonally across the joints to protect the grout, and rinse it frequently—very important—to keep it clean.

If your local tool rental dealer doesn't carry grouting machines, you can clean the tiles with a standard grout sponge and a pail of clean water.

Finishing Touches

Once you've cleaned the tile, allow the floor to dry for an hour or so. Then buff each tile with a dry, soft cloth to remove any remaining haze. Work carefully around the tile joints; the grout will be stiff, but not yet fully cured.

The glazed surface of the tile is impervious to staining, but the same isn't true for the grout, which is very porous. To help the grout resist discoloration and staining, apply a clear, silicone-based grout sealer.

PRO TIP

When caulk is cold it's very difficult to squeeze it out of its cartridge. Worse, though, caulk doesn't flow as smoothly or adhere as well when it's cold. So if you forget to bring the caulk indoors the night before (as I did), try this trick: Place the chilled cartridges in a sink of warm water and let them rest for 10 or 15 minutes.

Install shoe molding

On some installations, both the baseboard and shoe moldings are removed prior to tiling. On others, just the shoe molding is taken off. For our installation, the baseboard was left intact, so we just needed to replace the shoe molding.

The fastest, easiest way to install shoe molding—or baseboard—is with a pneumatic brad nailer, as shown in **A**. Press the shoe down tight against the tile, then shoot the nails into the baseboard.

Caulk joints

It's best to use caulk, not grout, to fill joints between the tile and other surfaces, such as cabinets, thresholds, and transition moldings. That's because these surfaces expand and contract with changes in humidity, and that slight movement can crack grout. High-quality silicone or siliconized caulk is flexible enough to accommodate a little expansion and contraction.

Use a caulking gun to apply a narrow bead of caulk between the tile and cabinets, as shown in **B**. Lightly wipe the bead smooth with a wet finger.

MARBLE TILE

From cottages to castles, natural stone has proven itself throughout many centuries to be a beautiful and remarkably durable flooring material. And to this day, natural-stone floors remain extremely popular for both new construction and renovation projects.

Floor tiles cut from granite, slate, limestone, and marble are readily available in an almost limitless number of colors, patterns, sizes, and textures. For the bathroom floor shown here, we set 12-in. by 12-in. tumbled marble tiles over cement backerboard. However, before setting the tile I took the opportunity to upgrade the room's heating system by installing a Nuheat® electric radiant-heat mat. This step is optional and can easily be omitted from the step-by-step tiling sequence.

It's worth mentioning that there are porcelain-ceramic tiles that look nearly identical to their natural-stone counterparts, and they often cost less. However, what manufactured tiles can't mimic is the completely random, incredibly beautiful, and truly unique subtleties that only Mother Nature can create. ▶ ▶ ▶

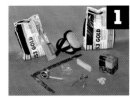
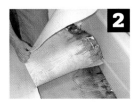

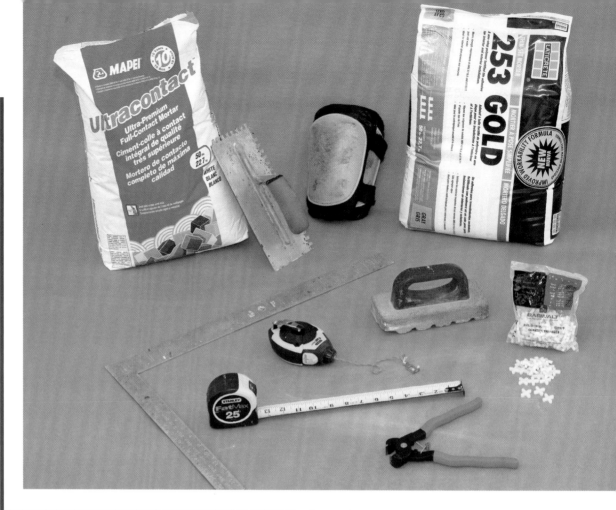

Basic floor-tiling tools include (back row) white thinset mortar, notched trowel, knee-pads, and gray thinset mortar. Also needed (front row) are a framing square, tape measure, chalk reel, rubbing stone to ease the edges of cut stone, tile nippers, and box of 3/16-in. rubber tile spacers.

Tools and Materials

Most of the tools and materials required for putting down a marble floor are identical to laying any tile floor, with two important exceptions: Marble, and all other natural stone tiles, can't be cut with a manual score-and-snap tile cutter; you must use a motorized wet saw, which you can rent by the day. The saw sits over a water tub that has a submersible pump, which delivers a stream of water that cools the blade and eliminates dust. Its toothless, diamond-impregnated blade can make precise straight, notched, and even curved cuts. Also, marble tiles must be set in white thinset mortar. Using standard gray mortar can cause the marble to warp and crack.

To install cement backerboard, you'll need (from the top) a T-square, notched trowel, impact driver or cordless drill, jigsaw and circular saw, margin trowel, self-stick mesh tape and 6-in. drywall knife, and a carbide-tipped scoring tool.

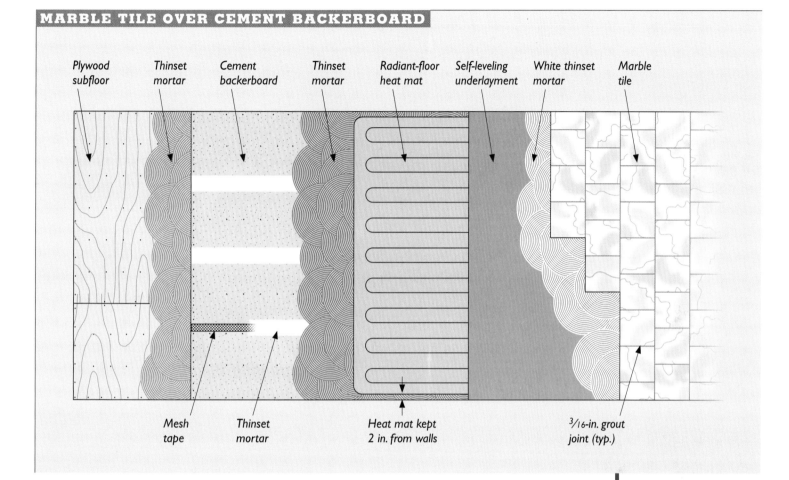

MARBLE TILE OVER CEMENT BACKERBOARD

Plywood subfloor

Thinset mortar

Cement backerboard

Thinset mortar

Radiant-floor heat mat

Self-leveling underlayment

White thinset mortar

Marble tile

Mesh tape

Thinset mortar

Heat mat kept 2 in. from walls

3/16-in. grout joint (typ.)

Keep in mind, too, that if you need to install cement backerboard prior to setting the marble, you'll need a few extra tools for cutting and fastening the backerboard to the plywood subfloor. If, however, the subfloor is at least 1¼ in. thick, you can skip the backerboard—if you'd like— and mortar the marble directly to the subfloor.

Take Up the Old Floor

The first step to putting down a new marble floor is removing all the moldings from around the room. If working in a bathroom, you'll also need to remove the toilet. In some instances you may be able to lay backerboard or plywood underlayment directly over the existing floor, but in this case it wasn't possible. Water had seeped under the old vinyl floor and rotted the plywood below. I had no choice but to tear up the vinyl and repair the damaged plywood subfloor.

Remove room moldings

Start by removing all transition moldings and baseboard moldings from the room. If you plan to reinstall the moldings after tiling, remove them carefully to avoid damaging them. It's also a good idea to label each piece, indicating its position in the room.

PRO TIP

If you're installing a radiant-floor heat mat or need to fill in low spots in the floor, pick up a bag of self-leveling underlayment, which is essentially very thin-viscosity cement.

How to Remove a Toilet

ONE OF THE FIRST STEPS TO tiling a bathroom floor is removing the toilet so you can tile the area beneath it. Fortunately, this is a very simple job, even if you've never before attempted a plumbing project. Here are the basic steps:

1. To start, reach behind the toilet and close the shut-off valve to stop the flow of water. Turn the handle in a clockwise direction.
   Then flush the toilet and hold down the handle, allowing as much water as possible to drain from the tank. Remove the top of the tank and use a sponge to sop up any water left in the bottom of the tank.

2. Take a 5-gal. bucket and fill it about halfway with water. Then, in one quick motion, dump all the water from the bucket into the toilet bowl, as shown in **A**. The pressure of all that water rushing into the bowl will force out most of the standing water.

3. Use a plastic or paper cup to scoop out as much of the remaining water from the bowl as possible.

4. Remove the last bit of water from the toilet with a large sponge. Wring out the sponge and repeat several times until you've sopped up all the water.

5. Disconnect the toilet's water-supply line from the shut-off valve by using a wrench to loosen the compression fitting, as shown in **B**.

6. Remove the plastic caps from the sides of the toilet's base to expose the two closet bolts. Use

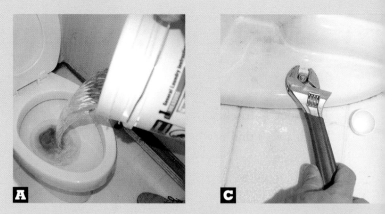

A

B

C

a wrench to remove the hex nuts from the bolts, as shown in **C**.

7. Spread a tarp or thick blanket on the floor in front of the toilet. Rock the toilet back and forth to break the seal with the closet flange (floor drain). Straddle the toilet and grab each side of the bowl close to the tank. Bend your knees, keep your back straight, and lift straight up. Set the toilet down on top of the tarp, as shown in **D**.
   Now use the tarp to drag the toilet from the room, but be sure to have a helper steady the toilet to keep it from tipping over. Finally, plug up the closet flange with an old towel to seal out sewer gasses and to prevent anything from dropping down the hole.

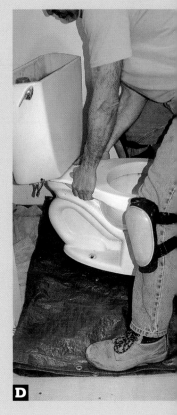

D

1. Use a pry bar to remove the metal or wood transition molding nailed across the doorway's threshold, as shown in **A**. If the transition molding is made of marble, remove it with a cold chisel and hammer.

2. Pry wooden baseboard moldings off the wall with a very thin pry bar. Slip a wood shim behind the pry bar to prevent the bar from denting the wall, as shown in **B**.

After removing the moldings, check the threshold and wall surfaces for protruding nails, which will often pull through the moldings. Remove any left-behind nails with pliers or a claw hammer.

Remove existing vinyl floor

As mentioned earlier, the plywood subfloor in this bathroom had suffered extensive water damage, so the vinyl sheet floor had to be removed. However, in most cases you can lay backerboard over an existing vinyl, laminate, or wood floor, if the flooring, subfloor, and joists are structurally sound and free of rot or damage.

1. Starting in the room corner, use pliers to grab hold of the sheet vinyl. Pull the flooring up and away from the corner, as shown in **C**. Fortunately most sheet vinyl flooring is glued down only around the room's perimeter. If yours is adhered to the entire subfloor, or if you're removing vinyl tiles, you'll have to use a long-handled floor scraper.

2. After loosening one corner, use a utility knife to score the surface of the flooring every 16 in. to 20 in. Don't worry about cutting all the way through the flooring; just score the

A

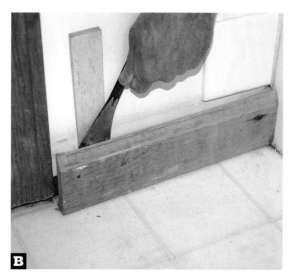

B

C

If you need to remove vinyl sheet flooring from a large room, use a hook-blade utility knife. Simply slide the sharpened hook under the flooring and pull. It'll quickly slice through the flooring without cutting into the subfloor below.

SAFETY FIRST

Resilient (vinyl) flooring manufactured prior to 1986 may contain asbestos, a known carcinogen. If at all possible, leave the old floor undisturbed and cover it with plywood or cement backerboard. If it must be removed, hire an asbestos-abatement contractor. Never scrape, sand, cut, or tear out asbestos-laden flooring.

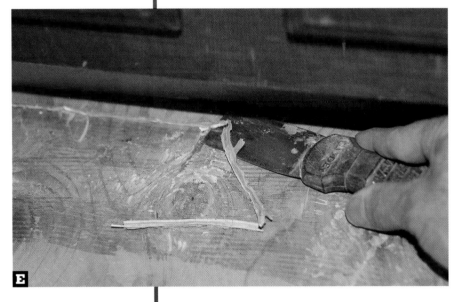

Patch the Subfloor

If you suspect that the subfloor might be damaged or compromised in any way, you must take the time to remedy the situation before proceeding. Laying marble tile—or any other flooring for that matter—over a weak, unsound subfloor will only lead to trouble. Cracked tiles are only one concern; you could end up with a sunken floor in need of expensive structural repairs. Don't risk it. Make the necessary repairs now and your marble tile floor will last for many years.

Pry up damaged plywood

In a bathroom, water damage often occurs alongside the tub, where water is regularly splashed onto the floor. (That's where I found extensive rot.) You might also find damage around the toilet base or beneath a pedestal sink. And keep in mind that most subfloors are made up of two layers of plywood or oriented strand board.

1. Start by using a circular saw to cut out the damaged section of plywood, as shown in **A**. Adjust the saw to cut only through the top plywood layer; ½ in. or ⅝ in. deep is usually sufficient. If possible, position the cut so it runs down the center of a floor joist. And be sure to cut well beyond any rot and into sound, dry wood.

2. Extract all nails and screws from the cut piece of plywood, then use a hammer and pry bar to pull it up.

3. Cut a slightly narrower section of plywood from the bottom layer of subfloor **B**. Again, be sure to cut only deep enough to go through the plywood; you don't want to cut into the joists below.

PRO TIP

To avoid damaging the sawblade when cutting through the plywood subfloor, remember to first remove all nails or screws along the cut line prior to sawing.

surface. When you pull on the flooring, it'll rip along the scored line, as shown in **D**.

3. Discard the old flooring and sweep the room clean. Then inspect the room perimeter for areas where vinyl flooring adhesive may have squeezed out from under the flooring. Use a narrow, stiff-blade putty knife to scrape up these dried ridges of glue, as shown in **E**. If you don't remove these obstructions, they'll interfere with the setting of the backerboard.

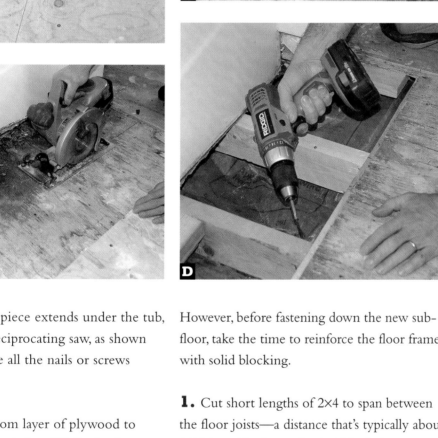

PRO TIP

Before sliding the plywood patch into place, mark the positions of the 2×4 blocking on the adjacent subfloor so you'll know where to drive the screws. Once the patch is in place you won't be able to see the blocking.

TRADE SECRET

When patching a subfloor, be certain to cut the replacement pieces from exterior-grade plywood, which is made with water-resistant glue.

4. If the plywood piece extends under the tub, cut it free with a reciprocating saw, as shown in **C**. Then remove all the nails or screws fastening it down.

5. Pry up the bottom layer of plywood to reveal the floor joists below. While the floor frame is exposed, it's important to keep all children and pets out of the room.

Install new plywood

Once you've cut out all the rotted sections of subfloor, you can cut new plywood pieces to fit.

However, before fastening down the new subfloor, take the time to reinforce the floor frame with solid blocking.

1. Cut short lengths of 2×4 to span between the floor joists—a distance that's typically about $14\frac{1}{2}$ in. wide. Space the 2×4 blocks between 12 in. and 16 in. apart, and secure them to the joists with $2\frac{1}{2}$-in.-long drywall screws, as shown in **D**.

2. Apply a thick bead of construction adhesive to the top edges of the 2×4 blocks. The adhe-

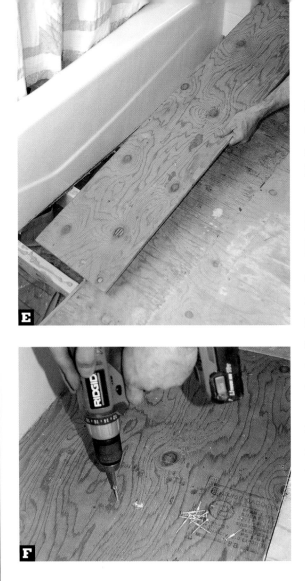

E

F

5. Apply construction adhesive to the surface of the just-installed plywood patch, then set down the top plywood layer. Fasten the top layer with 1⅝-in. decking screws, as shown in **F**.

Install Cement Backerboard

Cement backerboard provides the ideal substrate for setting tile. However, if the plywood subfloor is at least 1¼ in. thick you can skip this step and set the tile directly on the plywood. In this case, the subfloor was composed of two layers of ½-in. plywood, so I had to add a layer of ¼-in.-thick cement backerboard to obtain the recommended thickness of 1¼ in. With that said, regardless of the subfloor thickness, you should still consider installing backerboard; it'll create a rock-solid substrate and offer superior adhesion for your floor tile.

Cut the backerboard

There are a few different ways to cut cement backerboard, but the simplest, safest method is to use a carbide-tipped scoring tool. Backerboard contains silica dust, which can irritate lungs and nasal passages, so be sure to wear a dust mask when cutting backerboard.

1. Measure and mark the backerboard, then align a T-square with the cut mark. Draw the scoring tool along the edge of the T-square to scratch a groove into the surface, as shown in **A**. Repeat two or three times to deepen the groove.

2. Hold down the backerboard with one hand, making sure the scored line is facing up. Then pull up on the end of the sheet until it

sive isn't absolutely necessary, but it'll dramatically increase the hold-down strength of the screws and even help reduce floor squeaks.

3. Slide the bottom layer of plywood into place, as shown in **E**. Check to be sure it sits flat and flush with the surrounding subfloor surface.

4. Tap the plywood patch down into the adhesive using a hammer and protective board. Then fasten the plywood to the 2×4 blocks and floor joists with 1⅝-in. decking screws spaced 4 in. to 6 in. apart. The galvanized screws will resist rust and corrosion much better than standard drywall screws.

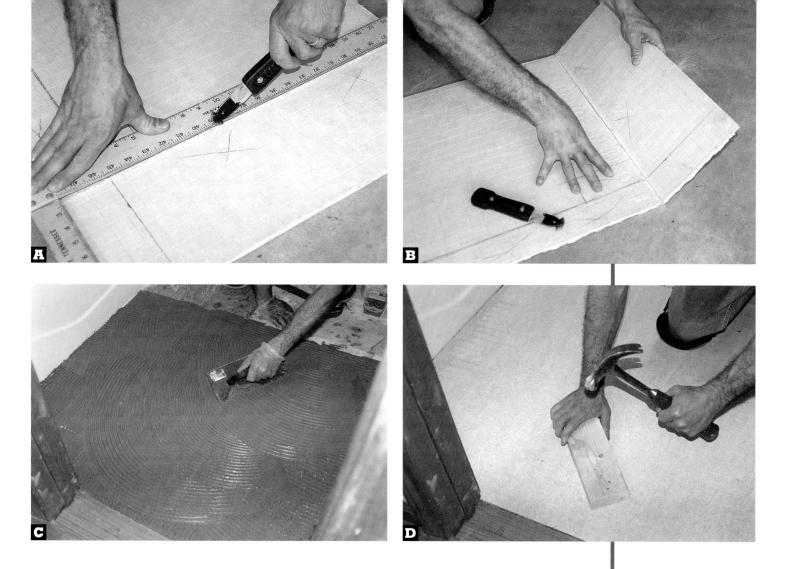

snaps in two, as shown in **B**. If the edge is a bit rough, pare it smooth with a utility knife.

Install the backerboard

Cement backerboard must be set down in a bed of thinset mortar to provide maximum support. Skip this step and you may save a little time, but you'll pay the price down the road when tiles start cracking and popping loose.

Use a latex-fortified thinset mortar and mix it with water until it's the consistency of yogurt—not overly stiff, but not runny either. The best way to mix mortar is in a 5-gal. bucket with a ½-in. electric drill fitted with a mixing paddle. Blend the mortar for six to eight minutes, then let it slake—or rest—for about 10 minutes prior to use.

1. Dump some thinset mortar onto the sub-floor. Use the smooth (un-notched) edge of the trowel to spread the mortar across the plywood. Then use the ¼-in. notched edge to rake the mortar smooth and even, as shown in **C**.

2. Set the backerboard into place, then use a hammer and 2×4 block to tap the backerboard down into the mortar, as shown in **D**.

3. Secure the backerboard to the subfloor with 1¼-in.- or 1⅝-in.-long backerboard screws. Be sure to follow the screw pattern marked on the backerboard sheet: Drive screws every 4 in. around the perimeter edges and space them 8 in. apart throughout the "field,"

Sawing Cement Board

USING A PORTABLE CIRCULAR SAW TO CUT CEMENT BACKERBOARD has certain advantages over using a scoring tool. First, the saw cuts more quickly and leaves a cleaner, smoother edge. It can also saw notches, plunge cuts, and inside corners much more easily than a scoring tool.

You don't need a special blade to cut backerboard; a carbide-tipped woodcutting blade works fine. However, you want a blade with the fewest number of teeth available. The blade I used had only four teeth, and it cut the backerboard like a hot knife through butter—very hard, dry, dusty butter.

A circular saw kicks up a cloud of dust, so be sure to wear a dust mask or respirator, and always cut outdoors; never use any power tool indoors to cut backerboard.

E

F

or center of the sheet. By the way, an impact driver provides the best and easiest way to drive the screws, but if you don't own one, use a standard cordless drill/driver.

4. Continue spreading thinset mortar onto the plywood subfloor with the notched trowel. Be sure the mortar extends beyond the edges of the sheet by at least an inch or two.

5. Set the backerboard into the thinset, making sure to leave a ⅛-in. gap between it and the neighboring sheet, as shown in E.

6. Fasten the sheet to the subfloor with backerboard screws, as shown in F. Again, follow the fastener pattern stamped into the surface of the sheet to ensure proper spacing between screws.

Set backerboard in toilet alcove

If you're tiling a bathroom floor, you'll have to install cement backerboard around the toilet's

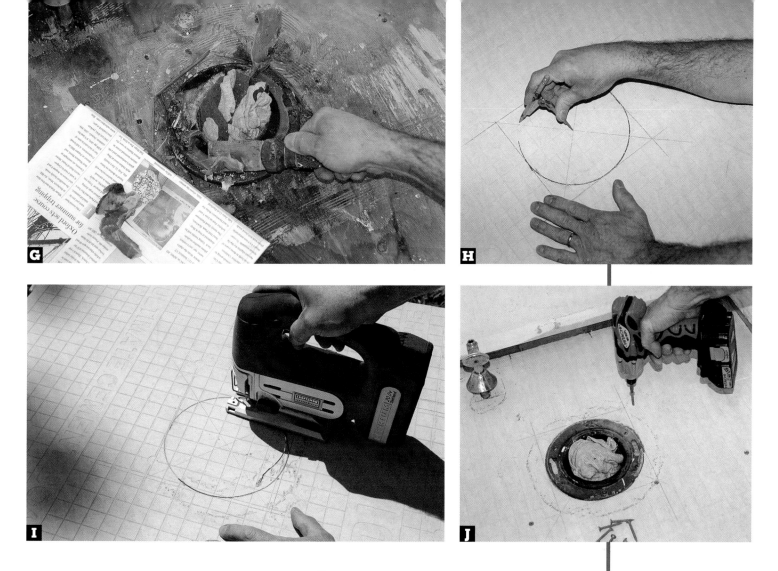

drain, which is called a closet flange. And if the shut-off valve protrudes from the floor, as most do, you'll have to notch the backerboard to fit around it, too. Fortunately, these cuts are easily made with a jigsaw fitted with a metal-cutting blade.

1. Start by using a putty knife to scrape the old wax seal from the closet flange, as shown in **G**. Place the sticky wax onto a sheet of newspaper and discard.

2. Use a pencil compass to draw a circle representing the diameter and position of the closet flange onto the backerboard, as shown in **H**. Make the circle about ¼ in. larger than the flange.

3. Cut the circle from the backerboard using a jigsaw fitted with a metal-cutting blade, as shown in **I**. Use moderate pressure—don't force the tool—and the saw will cut cleanly. Use the jigsaw to also notch the edge of the sheet to fit around the shut-off valve. Make all the cuts outdoors.

4. Use a notched trowel to spread thinset mortar onto the subfloor around the closet flange. Be careful not to get any mortar onto the surface of the flange or into the holes in the flange.

5. Set the backerboard down into the thinset and secure it with backerboard screws, as shown in **J**. Keep the screws at least 2 in. away from the circular cutout.

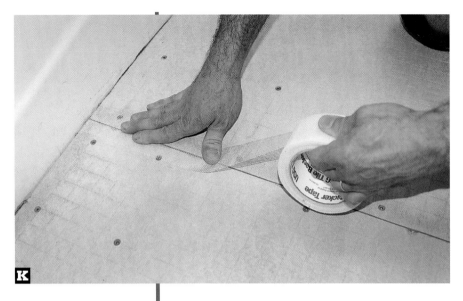

2. Adhere the mesh tape to the backerboard, making sure to center it over the seam between two sheets, as shown in **K**. Cut the tape to length with scissors or a sharp utility knife.

3. After taping all the seams, use a 6-in. drywall knife to spread a very thin layer of thinset mortar over the tape, as shown in **L**. Apply only enough mortar to cover the tape; avoid creating a raised hump along the seam.

Allow the taped seams to cure overnight before proceeding.

Install a Radiant-Floor Mat

At this point, with the backerboard seams taped, you can begin setting the marble tiles. However, if you'd like to upgrade the room's heating system, now's the time to install an electric radiant-floor heat mat.

The nice thing about sandwiching the mat between the backerboard and marble is that the entire floor will absorb and then radiate heat, creating a cozy, warm floor.

In a typical installation the mat is laid down in thinset mortar, more mortar is spread on top, and then the tiles are set. For this installation, however, I added a step to improve the performance of the radiant heat. I poured a thin layer of self-leveling underlayment (liquidity cement) over the mat and let it cure before setting the tiles. That extra cementitious layer provides a perfectly smooth, level surface for laying the tile and creates a bit more thermal mass for radiating heat.

For this installation, I ordered a custom-made mat from Nuheat, which perfectly conformed to the room layout. Standard size mats are also available. The mat comes with a thermostat and floor-sensing probe that relays the floor temperature to the thermostat.

Tape the joints

The final step to installing cement backerboard is to cover all the seams with adhesive-backed fiberglass mesh tape and thinset mortar. This is an important step because it creates a monolithic, seamless slab for setting the marble tiles.

1. Begin by wiping down the seams between the backerboard sheets with a damp—not wet—sponge. This simple action removes dust and grit, and ensures that the mesh tape will stick to the backerboard.

Set the mat in mortar

1. Begin by mixing up a batch of thinset mortar, making sure it's not too thin and watery. Starting in the far corner of the room, spread the mortar onto the backerboard with a ¼-in. notched trowel.

2. Lay the radiant-floor heat mat down into the mortar, as shown in **A**. Be careful not to crease or crush the electrical cables woven into the flexible mat.

3. Use a rubber grout float or thick, dense sponge to press the heating mat down into the mortar, as shown in **B**. It's important that the mat have 100-percent contact in the mortar.

4. Carefully fold the second half of the heating mat over the first half—don't crease it— then spread mortar over the backerboard, as shown in **C**.

5. Use the grout float to firmly press the mat into the mortar. Be sure to squeeze out all air bubbles and smooth any wrinkles.

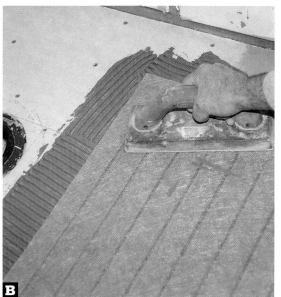

B

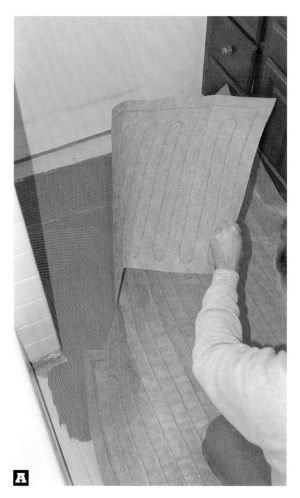

A

C

TRADE SECRET

To prevent the thinset mortar in the bucket from drying out—and to extend its working time— keep the bucket covered with a damp towel.

WHAT CAN GO WRONG

When spreading thinset onto the subfloor, you may occasionally feel the trowel hit a small bump or obstruction. Regardless of whether it's a dried glue blob or protruding screw head, be sure to remedy the problem or it'll prevent the backerboard from laying flat.

D

E

6. Cut a small slit in the mat and pull through the tiny floor-sensing probe, as shown in **D**. When slicing through the mat, be very careful to cut in the center between two electrical cables.

7. Pat down the mat with a damp sponge to ensure firm contact with the mortar. Pay particular attention to any areas where the mat has pulled away from the mortar. Allow the mortar to cure overnight.

F

Pour leveling compound

Mix up a batch of self-leveling underlayment according to the package directions. It should have the consistency of a milk shake: thick but pourable.

1. Starting in the far corner of the room, pour the underlayment directly from the bucket onto the floor, as shown in **E**. The thin cement will float out smooth and seek its own level.

2. If necessary, use a steel float to help spread the underlayment, as shown in **F**. Also use the float to feather out the underlayment around the edges of the electric heat mat.

Hook up the thermostat

The radiant-floor heat mat must be connected to a dedicated circuit. Hire a licensed electrician to connect the circuit to the main electrical panel, but you can do the rest of the work yourself, including pulling a new electrical cable from the panel and running the wires from the heat mat up inside the wall to the thermostat location.

1. Choose a spot on the wall for mounting the thermostat; it should be about 60 in. above the floor, between two studs, and well away from a window or vent. Hold an "old work" electrical switch box against the wall and trace around it. Use a drywall saw to cut the rectangular hole into the wall, as shown in **G**.

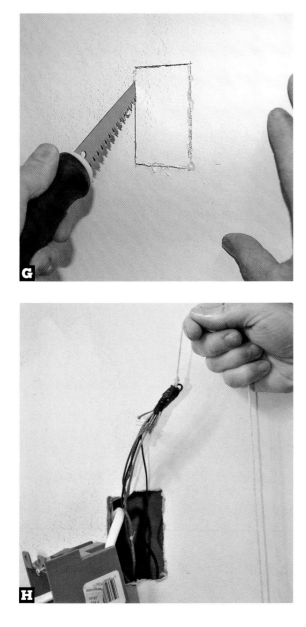

2. Pull a 14/2 nonmetallic electrical cable from the main electrical panel up the wall and through the switch box hole in the wall. Push the cable through the back of the switch box. Then pull the wires from the radiant-floor heat mat up through the hole, as shown in **H**. Installation methods differ, so always follow the manufacturer's instructions. Seek the advice of a licensed electrician if you are unsure of how to proceed with any wiring task.

3. Test the wires in the radiant-floor heat mat to ensure that they are working properly. To do this, use either a plug-in polarity checker with a ground-fault circuit interrupter receptacle testing feature or a manufacturer-specific electrical ground-fault indicator (like the one shown above). If you're using manufacturer's tester, connect the red wire to the "load" terminal and the silver ground wire to the "shield" terminal, as shown in **I**. If all is well, the alarm will sound and the "open circuit" indicator will light up. If there's a problem, the "ground fault" light will illuminate.

Set the switch box into the hole and press it flush against the wall. Tighten the two corner screws on the box until the box is held securely in place.

TRADE SECRET

Check the mat's wiring during installation, before laying tile. To make it easier to do so, route the heating wires and the thermostat wire before beginning to bed the mat in the thinset, and start bedding the mat at the point where the wires enter the wall.

4. Remove the faceplate from the thermostat and make the wire connections at the rear of the thermostat. Use twist-on wire connectors to join the red thermostat wire to the white cable wire; connect the black thermostat wire to the black cable wire. Connect the cable's bare copper ground to the silver braided metal sheathing.

Screw the thermostat to the switch box and connect the floor-sensing wires to the two front terminals, as shown in **J**.

5. Hook the faceplate onto the thermostat, as shown in **K**. Press the faceplate flat against the thermostat, then tighten the tiny screw on the bottom end to secure the faceplate.

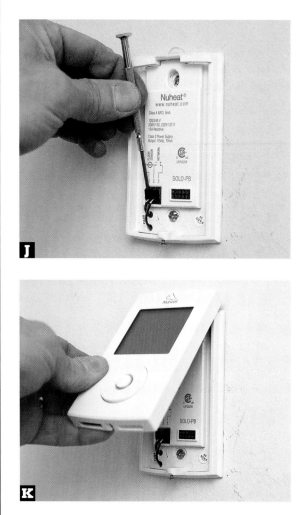

Install the Marble Tile

With the subfloor prepped, it's finally time to start setting the marble tile. Remember, you must use white thinset mortar specifically made for natural stone. But before mixing up any mortar, take the time to establish the tile pattern on the floor.

Lay out the tile pattern

Ordinarily it's recommended that you balance the tile pattern on the width of the room so the first and the last rows of tile are all the same size. However, for a bathroom or similar space it's best to balance the pattern on the most visually dominant area; in this case, the space between the vanity cabinet and bathtub.

1. Check to see if the tile fits under the door casings. If not, you'll have to trim the casings. Turn a tile upside down (to protect its finished surface) and set it down close to the door casing. Hold a handsaw flat against the tile and saw through the casing, as shown in **A**.

Remove the severed piece of wood and vacuum the area clean. Repeat for the remaining door casings.

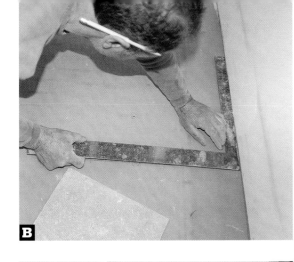

B

C

D

Start tiling

Once you've established the tile pattern you can mix up the mortar and—finally—begin laying tiles, starting at the room's centerline.

1. Mix white latex-fortified thinset mortar with water, then let it slake (rest) for about 10 minutes. Starting at the centerline snapped down the middle of the floor, spread about 4 sq. ft. of mortar onto the floor with a ¼-in. notched trowel.

2. Place the edge of the first tile right on the centerline and press it down into the mortar. Set the next couple of tiles, then apply more mortar, as shown in **D**.

3. To maintain consistent, uniform spaces between the tiles, insert ³⁄₁₆-in. rubber spacers between the tiles, as shown in **E** on p. 116.

2. Hold a framing square against the wall to form a perpendicular line along the floor, as shown in **B**. Set the square in the center of the room's main area and draw a layout line onto the floor.

3. Stretch a chalkline down the center of the floor, as shown in **C**. Align the string precisely with the perpendicular line marked on the floor, then snap the chalkline. This line will represent the center of the tile layout.

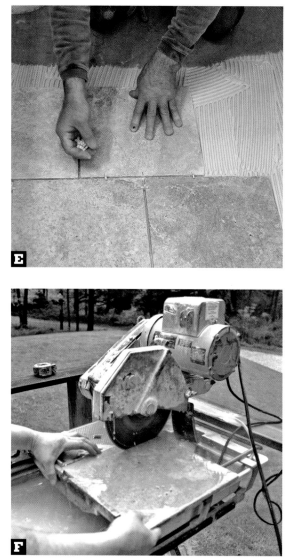

E

G

F

H

4. When you have to cut a tile, use the motorized wet saw. Place the tile onto the saw's sliding table, then push it forward into the blade, as shown in **F**.

Tiling around a closet flange

If you're tiling a bathroom, you'll need to cut tile to fit around the toilet's closet flange. You may need to cut just one tile (as I did) or two or three. It all depends on how the tile pattern falls at the flange. Regardless of how many tiles you need to cut, the wet saw provides an easy way to make the circular cutout.

1. Hold the tile to be cut in place and mark the position of the closet flange onto the tile, as shown in **G**.

2. Set a plastic flange extension ring onto the tile and use it as a template to trace the circular cutout, as shown in **H**.

3. Keep the rear edge of the tile tight against the wet saw's sliding table and tilt up the front

edge slightly. Slide the tile forward into the spinning blade, making the first cut along the outer edge of the circle, as shown in **I**.

Continue to make small cuts into the tile, removing material slowly.

4. Once you've cut away part of the tile, make several long, closely spaced cuts across the diameter of the circle, as shown in **J**.

5. Keep cutting away at the tile a little at a time until the circle is formed, as shown in **K**.

6. Hold the tile in place over the closet flange, as shown in **L**, but don't set it down into the mortar just yet. Check to be sure the tile will fit around the flange with a little room to spare. If necessary, bring the tile back to the wet saw and cut away a bit more material.

Finish tiling

1. Continue setting tiles across the floor, making sure to follow the pattern established earlier. Use the notched trowel to spread only about 4 sq. ft. of mortar at a time. That way you won't feel rushed to set the tiles before the mortar begins to harden.

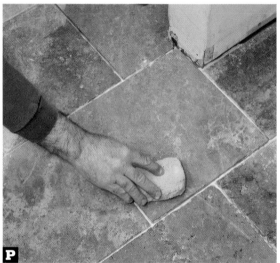

2. When tiling along a vanity cabinet, it's necessary to slip each tile underneath to the recessed toe kick, as shown in **M**. Be sure the mortar extends all the way to the toe kick so that the entire tile is bonded to the floor.

3. To tile around a doorway, you'll likely have to notch a few tiles. Cut the notches on the wet saw, then slip the tile under the door casings, as shown in **N**.

4. Cut the last tile to size and drop it into place, as shown in **O**. Insert spacers around the tile, then press it down flush with the neighboring tiles.

Allow the thinset mortar to harden overnight, then remove all the spacers from between the tiles.

5. Marble, like most natural stone, is very porous. To prevent staining and water spotting, use a sponge or white cloth to apply a coat of penetrating sealer to the tiles, as shown in **P**. Be sure to use a sealer specifically formulated for natural stone. Allow the sealer to dry overnight before grouting.

Grout the Tile

Welcome to the final tiling step: filling the joints between the tiles with grout. In this case, the grout joints were wider than ⅛ in. so I used sanded grout. For joints ⅛ in. or narrower, use nonsanded grout.

Be sure to use polymer-modified tile grout, which contains acrylic additives that make the grout much more water- and stain-resistant. The tool used to apply grout is called a rubber float or grout float, which is simply a flat rubber-faced trowel.

Spread the grout

1. Pour some grout into a small bucket. A little grout goes a long way, so only mix up a small amount. By the way, this is a good job to do outside or in the garage, because it's virtually impossible not to spill grout or splash water out of the bucket.

2. Add a little water to the bucket and mix the grout with a margin trowel, as shown in **A**. If the mix is too dry, add a bit more water. If it's too soupy, add more grout. The final blend should be the consistency of ultrasmooth peanut butter.

3. Using the margin trowel, scoop some grout from the bucket and plop it onto the floor. Use the rubber float to smear the grout diagonally across the tiles, forcing it deep into the joints, as shown in **B**.

4. Next, hold the float at an angle, press down hard, and pull the grout across the tiles, as shown in **C**. The goal is to fill the joints and wipe off the excess grout all in one motion.

5. Continue to work your way across the floor, checking frequently to make sure that you're completely filling each joint. For better leverage, try using the front edge of the float to press the grout into the joints, as shown in **D**.

Clean the tile

After grouting, wait 15 to 30 minutes before attempting to clean the tiles. You must wait long enough so that you can wipe the tiles clean without disturbing the grout. However, wait too long and the grout will harden on the tiles. Be aware that grout will dry much faster on a hot, dry day than on a cool, humid one.

Play it smart: Wait 15 minutes, then use a damp sponge to clean one or two tiles. If the sponge wipes the grout from the joints, stop, and wait another 10 or 15 minutes.

WHAT CAN GO WRONG

When cleaning grout from the tile, use a damp—not wet—sponge. If you flood the surface with water you'll dilute and soften the grout and create a weak grout joint.

1. For this job, I used a grouting machine to clean the tile, which is simply a large water bucket fitted with squeegee rollers. If you don't own a grouting machine or can't rent one, you can get good results with a large sponge and plastic bucket.

To use the machine, start by soaking a sponge float in the water bucket, then press it across the rollers to squeeze out the excess water, as shown in **E**.

F

2. The rollers remove most of the water, but the float is usually still a bit too wet. To remedy that problem, hold the sponge over the bucket and press your hand across the sponge to squeeze out the remaining water, as shown in **F**.

3. Hold the sponge float flat against the floor, apply moderate downward pressure, and wipe the tiles clean, as shown in **G**. After each pass, rinse the float in the water bucket.

G

Continue to work your way across the floor, one section at a time, until all the tiles are clean. Allow the floor to dry for an hour or two, then buff the tiles with a dry, soft cloth. Work carefully around the tile joints; the grout will be stiff, but not yet fully cured.

Add trim

Before installing baseboard molding, go around the room and locate each wall stud. That way you'll be sure to nail the baseboard to the wall studs, not just to drywall.

You can use an electronic stud finder, but I find it just as fast to use a hammer and finishing nail to locate the studs. Tap the wall with the hammer until you hear a dull thud sound indicating solid wood. Then, hammer the nail through the wall to pinpoint the exact location of the stud. Just be sure to drive the nail through the wall below the height of the baseboard. That way the holes will be hidden behind the molding.

1. Cut the baseboard molding to length and nail it to the wall, as shown in **H**. If you don't have a pneumatic finishing nailer, you can, of course, use a hammer and finishing nails. Just be sure to drive the nails into the wall studs. And if working in a bathroom, nail up the baseboard in the toilet alcove prior to installing the toilet. Otherwise you'll have to work around the toilet, which is no fun.

2. At the threshold to the room you'll need to install some sort of transition molding to span from the new marble floor to the floor of the adjoining room or hallway. In this case, I made an oak threshold, which I beveled to accommodate the thickness of the marble. The threshold was cut to length and glued and nailed down, as shown in **I**.

3. After fastening down the oak threshold, I applied two coats of polyurethane varnish.

Once you find a stud, mark its position by putting a small strip of masking tape on the floor right in front of the stud. Also, save yourself some time and trouble by painting or staining the molding prior to installation.

PROTIP

Use a high-quality
silicone or siliconized
caulk, not grout, to fill
gaps between the marble
tile and the bathtub,
cabinets, and moldings.
Grout can't expand and
contract with changes in
humidity. Caulk, on the
other hand, will stay
flexible without losing
its grip.

Prep the Closet Flange

After tiling a bathroom floor, you'll find that the
new floor is higher than the toilet's closet flange.
However, to ensure a watertight seal with the
toilet, the flange must be flush with or slightly
higher than the tile. To remedy this situation,
raise the level of the closet flange with a closet
flange extension kit.

1. Take the two closet bolts that come with
the extension kit and insert them into the slots
on either side of the closet flange, as shown
in **A**. Check to be certain the T-shaped head
of each bolt is trapped in the slot.

2. Apply a thick bead of adhesive caulk
around the entire top surface of the closet
flange, as shown in **B**. Note that during this
phase, the drain pipe is still plugged up with
a cloth.

3. Place one of the extension rings onto the closet flange, as shown in **C**. Press down on the ring to set it into the adhesive caulk. Check to see if the ring is flush with or slightly above the surface of the marble tile. If it's still too low, install another extension ring.

Trim Doors to Fit

More often than not, you'll need to trim the bottom ends of the doors to clear the new marble floor. Here's a quick, foolproof way to ensure you cut the doors to the proper size.

Take measurements

1. Rather than measure the height of the door or doorway opening, try this: Lay a piece of ½-in.-thick plywood on the floor near the doorjamb. Then measure from the bottom of the bottommost door hinge to the plywood, as shown in **A**.

2. Transfer this measurement to the door, as shown in **B**. Check to be certain you're measuring from the bottommost door hinge. You don't want to accidentally trim off the top of the door. Mark the door with a framing square, or better yet, a 4-ft. T-square.

Cut the doors

1. Lay a straightedge across the door, align it with your mark, then score the cut line with a sharp utility knife, as shown in **C**. Scoring the line will help prevent the saw blade from splintering the face of the door.

2. Use a portable circular saw to trim the door to size, as shown in **D**. In this case, I made the cut freehand, but if you'd feel more comfortable, clamp a straightedge guide to the door to ensure a straight cut.

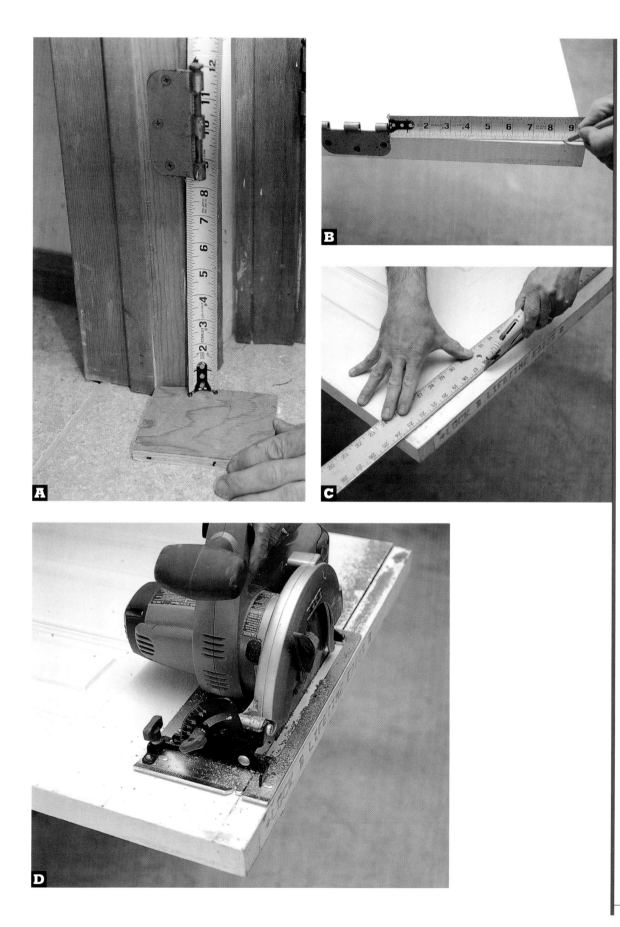

PLASTIC LAMINATE PLANKS

When Swedish flooring manufacturer Pergo first introduced plastic laminate flooring to North America in the mid-1990s, I was skeptical to say the least. Sure, plastic laminate was fine for countertops, but for flooring? I couldn't imagine a floor made of plastic laminate, and I was sure it would fail. Boy was I wrong.

Plastic-laminate planks represent the fastest-growing type of flooring sold today, and every major flooring manufacturer now offers laminate floors. The secret to its popularity and widespread acceptance is twofold: Plastic-laminate planks are extremely durable, highly stain-resistant, and easy to maintain, and they install with little effort, making them ideal for do-it-yourselfers.

Here, I'll show how to install 7½-in.-wide laminate planks that resemble traditional oak strip flooring. The 5/16-in.-thick planks are laid down over a thin underlayment and then snapped together–no glue or nails–to create a floating floor. It took less than four hours to lay the laminate floor in this 10-ft. by 12-ft. bedroom. ▶ ▶ ▶

Tools and Materials

One of the many advantages of installing a floating floor, such as laminate planks, is that you need very few tools. In fact, the newest laminate floors are so well engineered and snap together so easily, you could literally force them together with your bare hands. However, to save time—and wear and tear on your hands—you'll need a few simple hand tools to complete the installation.

To crosscut laminate planks, you can use a power miter saw, jigsaw, or portable circular saw. All the cuts will be hidden along the walls by shoe molding, so they don't have to be perfect. However, using a power tool creates quite a bit of dust; the core of the planks is made of medium-density fiberboard (MDF). For this job, I used a specially designed laminate-flooring cutter, which resembles a giant paper cutter. It's safe, quiet, and dustless, so it can be used right in the room where you're working without causing a mess.

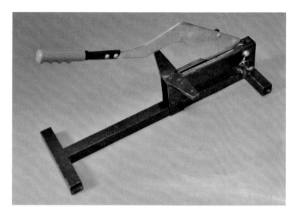

A laminate-flooring cutter provides a quick, quiet, and dustless way to crosscut the planks to length. The long handle creates the necessary leverage needed to cleanly slice through the hard $5/16$-in.-thick planks.

Tools required to install laminate flooring include (from top, left to right): reciprocating saw (or handsaw) for undercutting door casings and jambs, long tapping block, claw hammer, rubber mallet, roll of underlayment, pry bar, and tape measure. I'd also recommend a comfortable pair of kneepads.

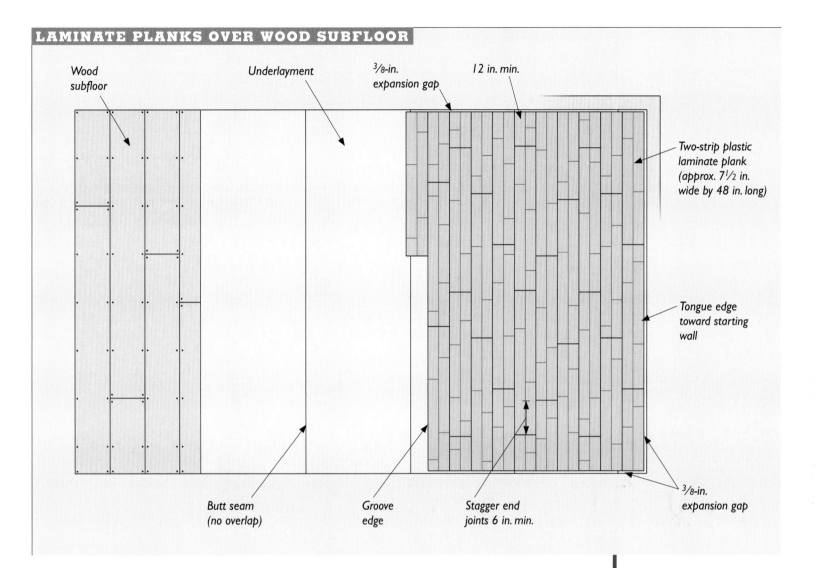

Wood subfloor

Underlayment

3/8-in. expansion gap

12 in. min.

Two-strip plastic laminate plank (approx. 7 1/2 in. wide by 48 in. long)

Tongue edge toward starting wall

3/8-in. expansion gap

Butt seam (no overlap)

Groove edge

Stagger end joints 6 in. min.

To rip planks lengthwise, you'll need a tablesaw (my preference), jigsaw, or portable circular saw. When ripping, it's best to set up the saw outdoors to avoid blowing dust all over the room.

Prep the Floor

Laminate flooring can be laid over most existing floors, as long as the surface is flat, smooth, and structurally sound. Unfortunately, this bedroom was carpeted, so the carpet had to be removed before we could proceed. Underneath was an old pine subfloor that was in surprisingly good

shape. A few loose and squeaky boards were screwed down to the joists, but because the laminate planks will float over the underlayment, no other prep work was needed.

Also, this room was trimmed with baseboard molding but no shoe molding. So we laid the flooring, leaving a 3/8-in. expansion gap around the room perimeter, and then concealed the gap with shoe molding. If your room has baseboard and shoe, remove the shoe before proceeding. If the room has neither baseboard nor shoe, then install the flooring, leaving a 3/8-in. gap at the walls. After the flooring is completed, install baseboard and, if you'd like, shoe on top of the floor, making sure you nail the moldings to the wall, not the flooring.

By the way, the installation shown here is suitable for most situations, including going over a plywood subfloor or existing hardwood, vinyl, or ceramic tile floor.

Undercut the door trim

1. Start by removing all doors from the room by popping out their hinge pins. Drop the pins into the doorjamb hinges for safekeeping.

2. You'll use a reciprocating saw or handsaw to trim the bottoms of the door casings and jambs so the laminate flooring can be slipped underneath. Stack a piece of underlayment and laminate plank in front of the door casing. Then step on the stack to prevent it shifting and slice through the casing with a reciprocating saw, as shown in **A**.

3. Rotate the underlayment-and-laminate stack around to the jamb and repeat the process. Continue in this manner until you've trimmed the casings and jambs on both sides of all the doorways in the room.

Install the underlayment

The underlayment used beneath laminate planks forms a moisture barrier and provides a cushioning layer. There are a few different types of underlayment available and they all work well, but it's important to use the type recommended by the flooring manufacturer. The underlayment must be suitable for your specific laminate floor and subfloor. In this case, we used a plastic-lined, felt-backed underlayment that came in 3-ft.-wide rolls.

1. Starting at one end of the room, roll out the underlayment, making sure it fits tight from

B

wall to wall, as shown in **B**. Use a utility knife to cut the underlayment to length. There's no need to staple or glue down the underlayment.

2. Roll out another length of underlayment and butt it tight to the first piece, but don't overlap it. Continue rolling out underlayment until you've covered the entire subfloor.

Start Flooring

Begin by measuring the width of the room to determine whether or not you need to rip down the planks in the first row. This is necessary to

avoid ending up with a narrow sliver of flooring along the far wall. It looks best if the first and last rows are about the same width, but it's far more important that neither row be less than half the width of one plank.

Here's how to calculate the width of the first and last rows: Subtract ¾ in. of expansion space from the room width, then divide by the width of each plank. That'll give you the number of full-width planks needed to cover the floor, plus the width of any remaining board. If the remaining board is less than half a plank, you must cut down the planks in the first row the appropriate amount. Be sure to rip off the tongue edge and keep the groove edge. For our installation, we didn't bother to rip down the first row because the last row ended being slightly wider than one-half of a plank.

It's necessary to stagger the end joints at least 6 in. from row to row. However, the completed floor will look much better if you stagger the end joints between 12 in. and 18 in.

Once you've installed the first two or three rows, the rest of the floor progresses pretty quickly. Notching around doorways will slow you down a bit, but most rooms only have two doorways.

It's also worth noting that most laminate planks can be joined together in two ways. The recommended technique is to insert one plank into the other at a slight angle and then press the first plank flat to the floor. However, you can also lay two planks flat against the floor and slide them together. The second method requires slightly more persuasion with the hammer and tapping block, but in some situations—such as around doorways—it's often the only way to join together two planks.

Another advantage of laminate planks is that you can work in two directions: tongue-to-

PRO TIP

Laminate planks snap together with very little effort. That's why it's much more effective to lightly tap them at several points along the edge, rather than pound on one spot with great force.

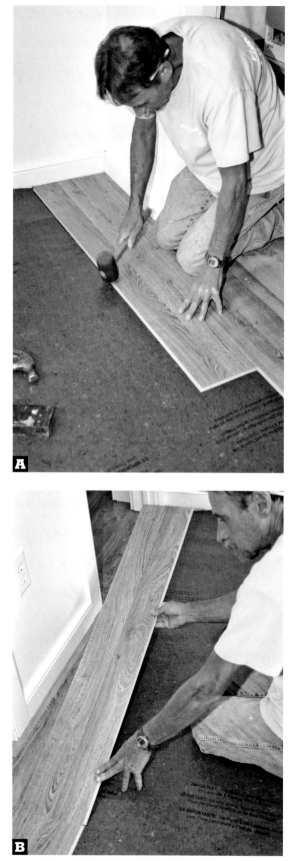

groove or groove-to-tongue. Again, it's easier to start with the tongue against the wall and groove facing out and then join the planks tongue-to-groove. However, when working parallel across the front of a closet or alcove, this dual-direction feature makes it possible to install planks in two directions: tongue-to-groove toward the room center and groove-to-tongue from the room into the closet or alcove.

1. Lay the first-row planks along the starting wall with their tongue edges against the wall and their grooves facing out toward the room center. To join planks end to end, hold one flat and raise the next plank at a slight angle. Press the ends together and lower the raised plank, and the tongue-and-groove end joint will snap closed.

If the end joint isn't perfectly tight, lightly tap the end of the plank with a hammer and tapping block. Cut the last plank in the first row to length, making sure to account for a ⅜-in. expansion space along the wall.

2. Set the first plank in the second row into place, making sure its tongue edge is pressed against the groove in the first-row planks. Angle the plank slightly to about 20 degrees, then press it flat to the floor. The tongue-and-groove joint will snap together. Use a rubber mallet to lightly tap the plank until it fits tight against the first row, as shown in **A**.

3. To install the second plank in the second row, butt it tight against the end of the previously installed plank, then raise it slightly, as shown in **B**. Lower the plank flat to the floor, keeping pressure in toward the mating plank.

4. Lift the edge of the plank slightly—just an inch is fine—and tap it with a rubber mallet, as shown in **C**. The long edge joint will snap closed.

5. Hold a tapping block against the plank end and lightly strike it with a hammer to tighten up the end joint between the planks. It's often helpful to press down on the end joint with one foot while tapping the block, as shown in **D**. That extra bit of pressure keeps the end joint aligned so it closes more easily.

Cut Planks to Fit

When you reach the end of each row of flooring, you'll have to crosscut a plank to fit. Again, the cleanest way to cut the planks is with a manual laminate cutter, but you can use a power saw as well.

If using a portable circular saw or jigsaw, cut the planks upside down so that any chipping will occur on the top, or back side, of the planks. Cut the planks faceup if using a power miter saw.

To reduce errors associated with measuring, it's much better to simply mark the planks that require cutting. Here's how:

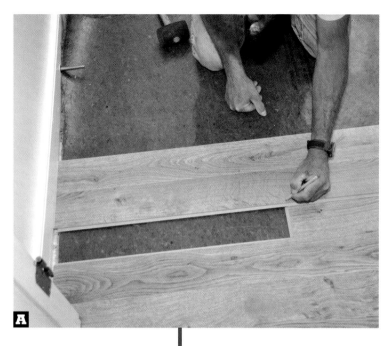

If you're not paying attention, it's easy to cut off the wrong end of a plank. To avoid mistakes, always place the end you wish to keep (usually the groove end) against the wall when marking the plank.

1. Lay a full-length plank in place with its groove end against the wall. Then mark where it meets the end of the previously installed plank, as shown in **A**. Be sure to allow for a ⅜-in. expansion space.

2. Cut the plank to length. If using a manual laminate cutter, hold the plank in place and lower the handle to start the cut. Then use two hands to press down until the blade slices through the plank, as shown in **B**.

3. When you reach the last plank in each row, snap then tap it into place, then use a pry bar to force closed the end joint, as shown in **C**.

The baseboard molding will provide proper support for the pry bar, but if you're working against drywall (no baseboard), slip a wood shim or board behind the bar to keep it from denting the drywall.

Stair-Step Technique

WHEN MOST DIYERS INSTALL LAMINATE flooring, they typically work back and forth plank by plank, one row at a time. And there's certainly nothing wrong with that technique, but professional flooring installers prefer the stair-step method because it allows them to work in one spot for longer periods before moving. Here's how:

A full-length plank is installed to start a row. Then, rather than installing another plank in the same row, a slightly shorter plank is used to start the next row. An even shorter plank is cut to begin the third row, and finally the shortest plank is installed in the fourth row, as shown at right.

Then, you shift down several feet and repeat this pattern for the second plank in each row, and then for the third plank and so on until all four rows are completed.

Fit Planks along End Wall

Upon reaching the end wall, you'll likely have to rip down the planks in the last row. Again, the easiest way to cut planks is with a tablesaw, but you could use a circular saw or jigsaw as well.

Rip planks to width

1. Adjust the rip fence on the tablesaw to the proper distance from the blade and lock it in place. When measuring to determine the width of the last-row planks, don't forget to take into account the ⅜-in. expansion gap.

2. Rip the last-row planks to width, as shown in **A**. Note that the planks are placed faceup when using a tablesaw. That's because the blade cuts in a downward arc, and any chipping will occur on the underside of the plank.

Install the Last Row

1. The easiest way to install the last row of flooring is to first snap together the planks end-to-end, as shown in **A**. What you are doing, in effect, is creating one long plank.

2. Slide the preassembled row into position, then carefully tilt it at an angle and pull it tight against the previously installed row, as shown in **B**.

3. Slip the pry bar behind the last row and then simultaneously pry against the baseboard

and tap the plank with the mallet, as shown in **C**. Slide the pry bar down a few inches and repeat until there's a tight seam along the entire row.

Install Shoe Molding

Assuming your room has its baseboard molding intact, as ours did, the next step is to install shoe molding around the room's perimeter to hide the expansion gaps.

If your room doesn't have trim, then start by installing baseboard. If the baseboard alone hides

C

A

the gap, which it should, then you don't have to install shoe molding as well, although it does help give the room a more finished look.

1. Cut shoe molding to fit from corner to corner and attach it to the baseboard—not the floor—with 1½-in. (4d) finishing nails. The quickest, easiest way to install the trim is with a pneumatic finishing nailer, as shown in **A**. Of course, you could also hand-nail the molding.

When installing shoe molding, cut miter joints at all outside corners and either miter joints or coped joints at all inside corners.

2. The last step is to determine if it's necessary to trim the bottoms of the room's doors so they clear the new laminate floor. Ideally you want at least ½ in. of space beneath each door. If necessary, cut down the doors with a portable circular saw.

RESILIENT SHEET VINYL

Resilient vinyl sheet flooring is decades old, and still commonly used in kitchens, baths, and laundry rooms. Its seamless, one-piece coverage is ideal for floors that are occasionally splashed with water. However, thanks to new colors and patterns, including ones that resemble hardwood planks and ceramic tile, it's not uncommon to see resilient vinyl in foyers, dining rooms, and bedrooms.

Here, I'll show how to install the latest generation of floating resilient vinyl over a plywood subfloor. Unlike earlier types of vinyl flooring, which had to be glued down, floating vinyl isn't adhered to the subfloor in any manner. This new easy-to-install sheet floor is much thicker and more durable than standard vinyl, resulting in a floor that lies flatter, lasts longer, and provides a soft, cushiony walking surface.

Vinyl sheet flooring comes in 12-ft.-wide rolls for seamless coverage in most rooms. However, I'll show how to seam two pieces of flooring to create an undetectable joint. The tile-look flooring shown here is Tarkett's FiberFloor in the Arizona Saltio pattern.

▶ ▶ ▶

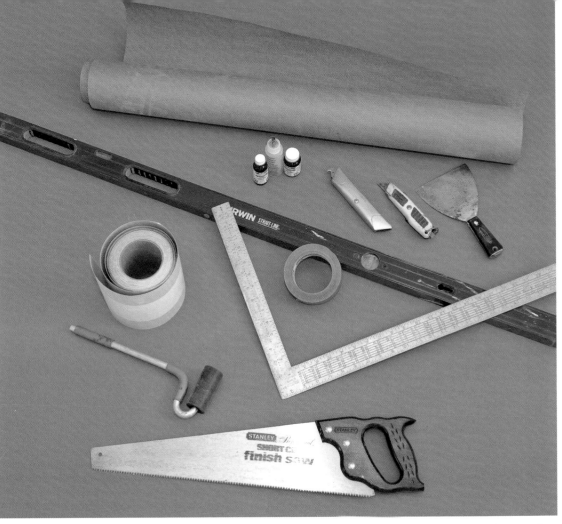

Installation of floating sheet vinyl requires (from the top): a roll of builder's paper; a two-part seam sealer; hook-blade and straight-blade utility knives; a drywall knife; a 6-ft.-long level; blue painter's tape; a wide roll of floating-floor seam tape; a framing square; a J-roller; and a crosscut handsaw.

Tools and Materials

The great thing about installing a new floating resilient vinyl floor is that you need only a few simple hand tools. If the plywood subfloor is squeaky and loose in places, you'll need a cordless drill/driver and some 1⅝-in.-long drywall screws to fasten down the plywood, but no power tools are needed to cut and install the flooring.

The two most critical steps occur before you ever lay down the new floor. First, be sure the subfloor is smooth and free of any obstructions, including protruding nail or screw heads, dried globs of paint or drywall compound, or raised splinters. Second, be sure to thoroughly sweep or, better yet, vacuum the subfloor clean of all dust, dirt, and grit, which, if not removed, will telegraph through the new flooring.

The tools required to lay a floating resilient vinyl sheet floor include a roll of builder's paper for making a template of the room; a two-part seam sealer for seaming two pieces together; hook-blade and straight-blade utility knives; a 4-in.- or 6-in.-wide drywall knife for scraping the subfloor clean; a 6-ft.-long level or similar straightedge; blue painter's tape for securing the paper template to the subfloor; a wide roll of floating-floor seam tape for seaming two pieces together; a framing square, which is used to make straight, square cuts; a J-roller for pressing down a seamed joint; and a crosscut handsaw for trimming doorjambs and door casings.

You'll also need a hammer and a thin pry bar to remove the shoe molding from around the room. The molding will be reinstalled, or replaced with new shoe, after the vinyl sheet flooring is installed.

Prep the Subfloor

Start by removing the shoe molding from around the room; you can leave the baseboard in place. If you plan to replace the shoe, remove it carefully to avoid breaking it.

It's best to remove the existing flooring, whenever possible, and start with a clean subfloor. However, if the floor is covered with old vinyl or linoleum you can save time by simply laying ¼-in. plywood underlayment over the old floor and then setting the new resilient sheet on top.

In cases where you decide to remove the existing floor, you'll most likely find a plywood

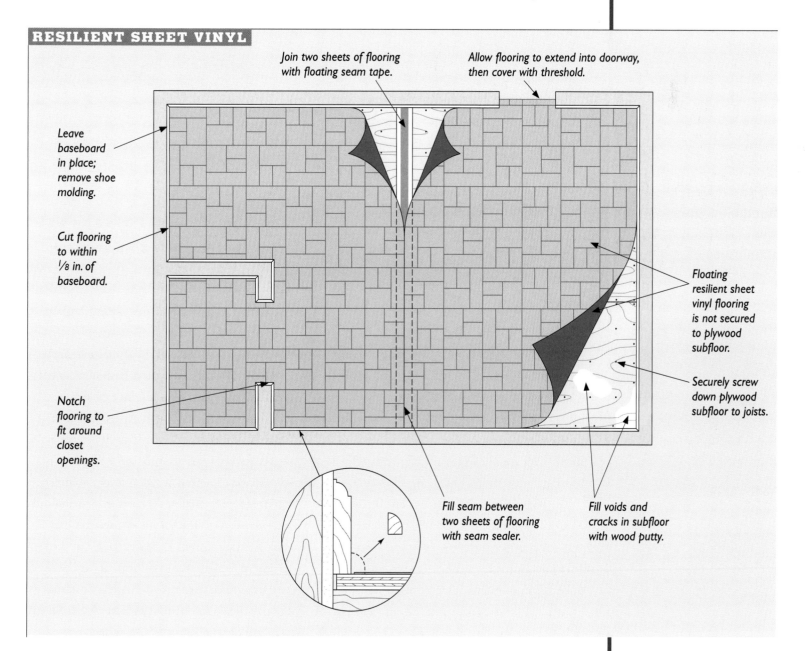

RESILIENT SHEET VINYL

Join two sheets of flooring with floating seam tape.

Allow flooring to extend into doorway, then cover with threshold.

Leave baseboard in place; remove shoe molding.

Cut flooring to within ⅛ in. of baseboard.

Notch flooring to fit around closet openings.

Floating resilient sheet vinyl flooring is not secured to plywood subfloor.

Securely screw down plywood subfloor to joists.

Fill seam between two sheets of flooring with seam sealer.

Fill voids and cracks in subfloor with wood putty.

A plywood subfloor will often have pieces of veneer missing from the top surface, which creates deep recesses. To prevent these defects from telegraphing through the new floor, fill all recesses, holes, and gaps larger than ⅛ in. with wood putty. Once the putty dries, sand the area flush.

subfloor beneath, as shown here. You can lay the new vinyl sheet directly over the plywood, but first you've got to make sure the surface is flat, smooth, and clean.

Check subfloor for obstructions

As mentioned earlier, it's important to clean the subfloor of all debris and obstructions before laying down the new sheet flooring. The amount of work it'll take to create a clean, smooth surface depends on the condition of the existing subfloor.

1. Use a 4-in.- or 6-in.-wide drywall knife to carefully scrape the subfloor clean of dried joint compound, paint, and other surface obstructions, as shown in **A**.

2. Then, use a hammer to pound all protruding nail heads flush with the plywood surface.

   If the plywood is screwed down, set offending screws below the surface with a cordless drill/driver. Remember that even tiny obstructions will eventually show through the new flooring.

Trim doorjambs

Resilient flooring is one of the thinnest floorings made, but even so, you may need to trim doorjambs and casings to allow the flooring to slip underneath.

1. Take a piece of cardboard or hardboard (Masonite) that's approximately the same thickness as the new vinyl floor and place it in front of the doorjamb. Then, lay a handsaw on top of the cardboard and saw through the jamb, as shown in **B**. Remove the cardboard and severed piece of jamb and you'll have a gap wide enough to accommodate the flooring.

2. Finish up by vacuuming the subfloor clean.

Make a Paper Template

If you've got a perfectly square or rectangular room, you could simply measure and cut the flooring to fit. But that's seldom—if ever—the case. Few rooms have precisely square corners and most have closets, doorways, built-ins, or cabinets that you must fit the flooring around.

That's why it's highly recommended that you make a paper template of the room and then use the template to mark the cut lines onto the flooring.

For the template, I used inexpensive builder's paper, which is sold in 3-ft.-wide rolls at most home centers. (Not to be confused with black builder's felt or building paper, used under roofing.) You could use narrower paper, even newspaper, but the wide sheets are more rigid, they don't rip as easily, and they transfer the room shape to the flooring more accurately.

1. Start in one corner and roll out about 6 ft. of paper, as shown in **A**. The end of the paper doesn't have to be tight against the baseboard; any gap will be covered by the next paper sheet. However, it's important to align the long edge of the paper very close to the baseboard, within 1/8 in. or so.

2. Use a straight-blade utility knife to cut a 2-in.- to 3-in.-long V-shaped flap into the paper, as shown in **B**.

Ice Scraper Saves Time and Toil

THE ROOM WHERE I INSTALLED this resilient vinyl flooring had recently been renovated with new drywall and paint. As a result, the plywood subfloor was a mess. Its surface was covered with small pools of dried paint, stuck-down pieces of masking tape, and rock-hard blobs of joint compound.

I started scraping the plywood clean with a 6-in.-wide drywall knife, which worked well, but I quickly realized that it would take too long to do the whole floor in this manner. So I went out to the garage and found a long-handled ice scraper, which is used to clean snow and ice from walkways and patios. It was the perfect tool for scraping the subfloor clean. It provided plenty of leverage to dislodge the largest, hardest mounds, and I was able to do it while comfortably standing upright.

The scraper's wide blade is also helpful in finding raised nail and screw heads. Just push the blade across the floor and listen for the distinctive "clang" when it hits a protruding fastener.

A long-handled ice scraper makes short work of scraping clean a plywood subfloor.

A

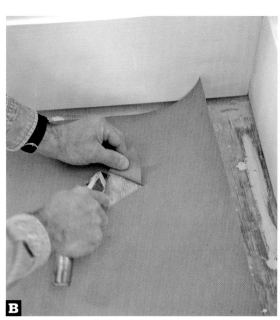

B

PROTIP

If you can't find builder's paper to make the template, you can use white butcher's paper, red rosin paper, or brown kraft paper. I prefer builder's paper because it comes in long rolls and costs less than the other options.

C

D

E

F

3. Fold over and press down the V-shaped paper flap to expose a triangular piece of the subfloor. Then adhere the paper template to the subfloor by pressing a strip of 2-in.-wide painter's tape over the cutout, as shown in **C**.

4. Continue rolling out the paper template along the wall. Cut V-shaped slices into the paper every 4 ft. or so, and stick down the paper with tape strips. When you reach the far wall, cut the paper end to within an inch or so of the baseboard. Again, an overlapping sheet of paper will cover the gap.

5. Go back to the starting point and unroll another sheet of paper along the adjacent wall, as shown in **D**. Keep the long edge within ⅛ in. of the baseboard, and align the end with the edge of the previously installed paper sheet.

Cut V-shaped slits into the paper and tape it down to the subfloor.

6. When you come to a closet door or other doorway, cut short pieces of paper to wrap around the wall, as shown in **E**. This is much easier than trying to accurately notch one large piece of paper.

7. Cut another short piece of paper to fit along the opposite side of the wall, inside the closet, as shown in **F**. Then continue the template around the inside of the closet using the paper roll. Note that depending on the size of the closet, you might have to slice the 3-ft.-wide sheets down to a narrower size.

Trace the Template onto the Flooring

The next step after making a template of the entire room is to lay the paper template on top of the vinyl flooring and then trace around it with an indelible marker. If you don't have space in the room to unroll the flooring, move it to a bigger room, garage, driveway, or other large, flat, clean surface.

1. Lift the paper template from the subfloor, being careful not to tear it. Fold the template into a manageable size.

2. Set the template in the middle of the vinyl flooring, then unfold it. Align one corner of the template with the flooring, keeping it about an inch or so inside the edge of the flooring, as shown in **A**.

Be sure the edge of the template is parallel with the pattern lines in the flooring. Also check to see that the other edges of the template fall on the flooring. Shift the position of the template, if necessary. Press down on the pieces of tape covering the triangular cutouts to adhere the template to the flooring.

3. Stick down the perimeter edges of the template to the flooring with small loops of painter's tape, as shown in **B**. Space the tape loops about 2 ft. apart around the entire template, making sure you smooth out all wrinkles.

4. With the template securely adhered to the flooring, use a medium-width indelible marker to trace around the paper template, as shown in **C**. The line doesn't have to be perfectly straight; just be sure to follow the template.

A

B

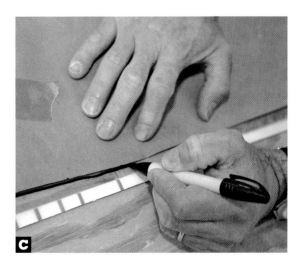

C

TRADE SECRET

Before tracing the template onto the flooring, check to be sure the template is taped down perfectly flat. If you see any wrinkles, smooth them out first.

D

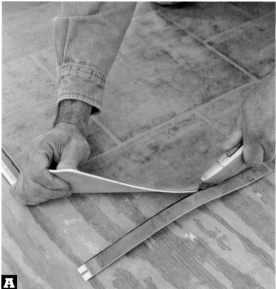

A

B

5. Use the marker to also trace around any notches that you must cut into the flooring so it'll fit around a doorway, as shown in **D**.

Cut the Flooring to Size

Once you've traced the outline of the paper template onto the vinyl flooring with a marker, remove and discard the template. Now prepare to cut the flooring to size using a utility knife fitted with a brand-new hook blade.

There's no real trick here—just cut along the marked lines. However, do proceed with caution and pay attention. One small slip from an instant of inattentiveness, and you can ruin the entire sheet of flooring.

1. Starting in one corner, slip the knife's hooked blade over the edge of the flooring and pull it toward you, as shown in **A**. You'll initially feel some resistance, but once the blade starts to cut, it'll slice through the flooring quite easily. Try to cut right down the center of the line. Keep steady pressure on the knife, but cut slowly to avoid careening wildly off course. And don't worry if the cut isn't perfectly straight, as the shoe molding will hide it.

2. Continue to cut along the lines around the perimeter of the sheet flooring. Then go back and use the hook-blade knife to cut the notches for any doorways, as shown in **B**. However, be very careful when cutting inside corners with the hook blade. If you pull too hard as you approach the corner, it's easy to cut beyond the line. I find it best to use the hook blade for the long, straight cuts, then switch to a straight-blade utility knife to cut through the flooring at the inside corners.

Lay the Flooring

Before carrying the cut-to-size flooring into the room where it'll be installed, vacuum the subfloor clean one more time. This is your last opportunity to ensure the surface is free of all debris. Also check your shoe soles for pebbles or caked-on dirt so you don't mess up the clean floor.

Loosely roll up the flooring and have someone help you carry it into the room. It's fine if the flooring bends a little, but be careful to support the roll to prevent it from bending sharply in the middle.

Once the flooring is placed in the room, installation only takes a matter of minutes. Don't forget this is a floating floor: no glue, no staples required.

1. Set the flooring down at one end of the room and unroll it across the subfloor. Carefully lift up the corners and flop each one down close to the wall (see the photo on p. 138).

Go around the room and check the fit of the flooring along the walls and around the doorways. If you need to shift the flooring for a better fit, lift up one corner, stand on the sub-

Vinyl Sheet Cutting Tools

THE TOOL MOST OFTEN USED to cut resilient sheet flooring, the hook-blade utility knife, is still the best tool to use. The inside crook of the hook is razor sharp, but its curved outer edge is not. That allows you to slice through the flooring without cutting into the subfloor below.

I also tried cutting the flooring with a pair of cordless electric scissors and was shocked to find that they worked. The 3.6-volt tool labored a bit, but it never stalled and left behind a perfectly clean edge. It was also easy to control and virtually impossible to accidentally steer off course.

The hook blade easily slices through resilient flooring; just be sure to start with a fresh blade.

Cordless, battery-powered scissors provide a very safe, user-friendly way to cut sheet flooring. Be sure to keep the tool plugged into its charger when not in use.

Before laying down the flooring, it's important to sweep or vacuum the subfloor clean of all dust and debris. Pay particular attention to the area along the bottom of the baseboard. The small gap beneath the molding can trap dirt that could end up under the new floor. Clean underneath the baseboard with a narrow crevice tool attached to a vacuum.

floor, and tug the flooring into position. The bottom surface of the flooring is rather slick, so even large sheets can easily be shifted around.

2. Be particularly careful when fitting the notched flooring around doorways. Fold back half of the notched section, then slide the flooring up to the wall, as shown in **A**. Gently set the folded section of flooring down on the back side of the wall; avoid sharp bends that could permanently crease the flooring. Be sure to slide the flooring beneath doorjambs and casings, where there won't be any shoe molding to hide the edge.

3. Go around the perimeter of the room and check once again the final fit of the flooring. If you find any spots where the flooring is fitting too tightly, carefully trim away the excess with a hook-blade utility knife, as shown in **B**.

Seam Two Pieces of Flooring

As mentioned earlier, vinyl sheet flooring comes in 12-ft.-wide rolls that are hundreds of feet long, so seaming two pieces together is only necessary in very large rooms. However, if you do need to seam together two pieces, you can take solace in the fact that the process is relatively simple and the results, if done correctly, will produce an absolutely undetectable joint.

Align the two sheets

The first step in seaming vinyl flooring is to align the two pieces to ensure the patterns printed on each piece match up perfectly. This is a bit difficult because you must overlap the two sheets before simultaneously slicing through both. And you can't see if the patterns are

A

B

aligned once the top sheet overlaps the bottom sheet. The trick is to cut "viewing windows" into the top sheet.

1. With the first (bottom) sheet of flooring installed, slide the second (top) sheet into position, but keep it pulled back a few inches from the edge of the first sheet. Next, use a straight-blade utility knife to cut 2-in.- to 3-in.-wide notches—known as viewing windows—into the edge of the top sheet, as shown in **A**. Note that it's important when cutting the viewing windows that you carefully position the cut that runs parallel with the mating edge precisely on the edge of a grout joint or other pattern line. Space the notches 3 ft. to 4 ft. apart along the entire length of the mating edge. (Do *not* notch the bottom sheet.)

2. After cutting all the viewing windows, pull the top sheet over the bottom sheet and shift it, as necessary, to align the pattern along the viewing windows with a matching pattern line on the bottom sheet, as shown in **B**.

B

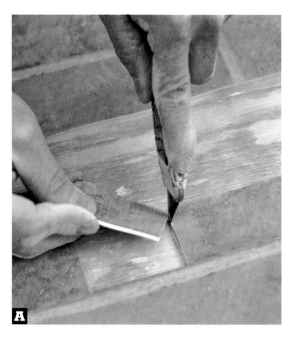

A

3. Once satisfied with the position of the top sheet, secure it in place with several strips of tape.

Seam the joint

To seam together two sheets of flooring, you must double-cut the joint, which just means slicing through both layers at the same time, and then removing the excess trimmed off both pieces.

To ensure an accurate, tight-fitting seam, be sure to use a long, perfectly straight guide, such as a 6-ft. level or similar straightedge, and a brand-new straight blade in your utility knife.

TRADE SECRET

When executing a double-cut through two layers of flooring, hold the knife perfectly vertical. If you angle the blade even slightly you'll end up beveling the cut, making it difficult to produce a tight-fitting seam.

When positioning
floating seam tape underneath the flooring, check the protective backing strip to make sure it's clean. If necessary, wipe it down with a damp cloth. Should dust or dirt fall from the backing strip during removal and land onto the exposed adhesive surface, the tape won't adhere to the flooring as well.

TRADE SECRET

Don't own a J-roller?
Get one. There's simply no faster, better way to firmly press the flooring down onto the seam tape. Some people suggest using a rolling pin, but forget it. It doesn't work. Spend the $15 or so for a 3-in.-wide J-roller. It'll be well worth it. Plus, you can use the roller for pressing down plastic laminate, veneer edge banding, and other thin materials.

C

D

You'll also need a roll of floating seam tape and some liquid seam sealer; both products are available at resilient flooring dealers.

1. Set the edge of the level directly over the center of the overlapping pattern lines. Kneel on the level to prevent it from moving (this is very important), and then slice through both flooring layers in one motion, as shown in **C**.

Slide the level down and align it precisely with the first cut and centered over the pattern line. Then make another cut through both layers. Repeat as many times as necessary to double-cut the entire length of the joint.

2. Slide the excess flooring cut from the top sheet out of the way, then reach underneath to carefully pull out the strip trimmed from the bottom layer, as shown in **D**.

3. Fold back the edge of the second sheet and unroll a length of floating seam tape along the joint. Cut the tape about 2 in. longer than the joint.

4. Lift up the edge of the flooring and slide the floating seam tape halfway underneath, as shown in **E**. Be sure the edge of the flooring runs down the middle of the tape.

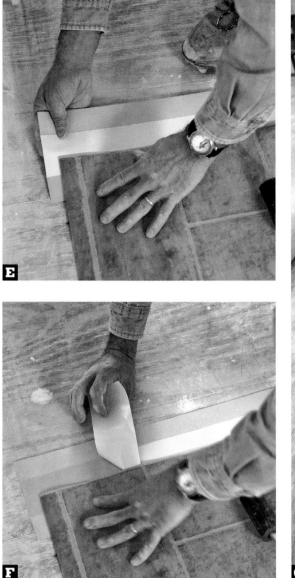

5. Now, pressing down on the flooring with one hand to prevent the tape from shifting, use your other hand to peel off the center backing strip and expose the sticky adhesive, as shown in **F**.

6. Continue peeling off the backing strip all the way down the entire length of the seam. Again, be sure to press down on the flooring to prevent the tape from shifting out of position.

7. To ensure a strong bond between the flooring and the tape, use a J-roller to forcefully press the edge of the flooring into the adhesive, as shown in **G**.

8. Next, slowly and very carefully lay the second sheet down alongside the first sheet, as shown in **H** on p. 152. Be sure to butt the two sheets tightly together along the seam. If necessary, ask someone to help you position the flooring during this phase.

9. Once the two sheets of flooring are butted together, use the J-roller to press the second sheet down into the seam tape, as shown in **I**. Then roll down the center of the seam, simultaneously pressing down both flooring edges.

Seal the seam

It's important to permanently seal the seam between two sheets of flooring, even if the joint is very tight. If you don't, dirt will accumulate along the joint, making the seam very obvious, and moisture will seep between the sheets and loosen the seam tape.

The best way to fill the seam is with two-part liquid seam sealer. Just be sure to use a sealer recommended by the flooring manufacturer, and

mix and apply it as directed. Also, keep in mind that a little seam sealer goes a long way: Two ounces of liquid sealer will fill about 75 linear feet of seam.

1. Vacuum along the seam to remove any dirt or grit. Then use a slightly dampened paper towel to wipe the seam clean of all dust. Wipe the seam dry with a clean paper towel.

2. Place the plastic applicator bottle on a flat surface and add equal amounts of Part A and Part B solutions. Again, be sure to read the package directions carefully; I had to shake Part B for 30 seconds before pouring it into the bottle, but didn't have to shake Part A at all.

Tightly twist the cap onto the applicator bottle, making sure the metal nozzle is firmly seated in place. Gently swirl—do not shake—the bottle to thoroughly blend together the solutions. (Shaking introduces air bubbles into the sealer.)

3. Use your forefinger to force the tip of the nozzle into the seam between the two sheets. Gently squeeze the bottle, then slowly pull the tip along the seam to apply the sealer, as shown in ▮. The goal is to overfill the seam slightly by applying a band of sealer that's about ³⁄₁₆ in. wide. It's important that the sealer bridges the seam and overlaps onto the edges of the two pieces of flooring.

4. Most seam sealers require 24 hours to fully cure. To protect the newly sealed seam, place strips of blue painter's tape along both sides of the seam. The tape will serve as a visual reminder to not step on the seam.

Once the sealer has cured, pull up the tape and install shoe molding around the perimeter of the room. Be sure to nail the shoe to the baseboard, not to the flooring.

PRO TIP

At the end of the installation, be sure to save any leftover flooring in case you ever need to make a repair. Scrap pieces of resilient flooring also make excellent—and extremely durable—car mats, shelf liners, and shop floor mats for use in front of workbenches and stationary woodworking machinery.

PRO TIP

To keep a resilient floor in like-new condition, vacuum it regularly to remove harmful grit, and damp-mop occasionally to clean off surface stains and dirt. Never use an abrasive cleanser on a resilient floor; it won't damage the flooring, but it'll scrub off the factory-applied sheen. Also, cleaners specifically formulated for resilient flooring are sold at most flooring dealers.

VINYL TILE

In many respects vinyl tile can't compete with vinyl sheet flooring. Sheet vinyl is faster and easier to install, provides seamless coverage, and comes in many more stylish patterns and colors. You might be wondering why anyone would consider vinyl tile. Here are two excellent reasons.

First, vinyl tile is much harder and more durable than vinyl sheet flooring. A properly installed, high-quality vinyl tile is virtually impossible to rip, gouge, or wear through. Second, vinyl tile allows you to mix and match colors and patterns to create a truly custom floor, with borders, inlay designs, alternating stripes, or checkerboards.

The most DIY-friendly of all vinyl tiles are the peel-and-stick type, which you simply press down to the subfloor. However, here I'll show how to install commercial-grade vinyl composition tiles (VCS) on a concrete slab using epoxy adhesive. This method requires more work, but it's absolutely the very best way to ensure a professional-quality, long-lasting job. ▶ ▶ ▶

Like other types of flooring, vinyl tile comes in a wide range of prices. It's important to buy the very best tile you can afford. Expensive tiles not only last longer and look better, but they're also much easier to install. That's because cheap tiles aren't consistently square, making it impossible to create tight joints between the tiles.

WHAT CAN GO WRONG

The epoxy bond will be compromised if it's applied over a dusty concrete slab. Damp-mop the slab clean and then let the floor dry completely before applying the epoxy.

The tools needed to install vinyl composition tiles include (left to right from top): a tape measure, a manual vinyl tile cutter, a chalk reel for snapping layout lines, a framing square for dividing the floor into quadrants, an electric heat gun, a utility knife for notching tiles, and a comfortable pair of kneepads, preferably the gel-filled kind.

To permanently adhere vinyl composition tiles to a concrete slab, you'll need (from left to right): a 1/16-in.-wide by 1/16-in.-deep notched trowel, rubber gloves, and two-part epoxy adhesive. The bucket contains the epoxide resin, and the bottle contains the polyamine catalyst, or hardener. The hardener is poured into the bucket of resin and mixed to create a thermosetting polymer adhesive, commonly called epoxy. The coverage rate for the epoxy shown is approximately 125 sq. ft.

Tools and Materials

The thing I like best about installing vinyl tile is that it's a very quiet, methodical endeavor. There are no power tools or saws needed, and you don't end up making a huge mess. It's also an uncomplicated installation; it's just the tiles, the adhesive, and you. OK, you do need a few hand tools, but only a few. And there's one specialty tool that you'll need, a manual vinyl tile cutter, which you can rent at any well-stocked tool rental dealer.

Prep the Room

It's important to begin with a dry, clean surface, so start by sweeping and then vacuuming the concrete slab to remove all dust and dirt. Then scrub off any stains with the appropriate cleanser or degreaser. The slab doesn't have to be sterile, but it must be free of all grit, grime, and grease.

The next step is to divide the room into quadrants by snapping layout lines with a chalk reel. Then you can begin spreading epoxy and laying tiles, one quadrant at a time.

Mark layout lines

1. Measure the width of the room and mark its centerpoint at two locations. Then snap a chalkline down the center of the room, as shown in **A**.

2. Measure the length of the room and mark its centerpoint on the chalkline. Lay a framing square on the chalkline at the centerpoint and draw a line along the square, perpendicular to the chalkline. Flip over the square and repeat

to draw a perpendicular line in the opposite direction.

3. Now stretch the chalkline across the line already marked on the floor, aligning it perfectly

A

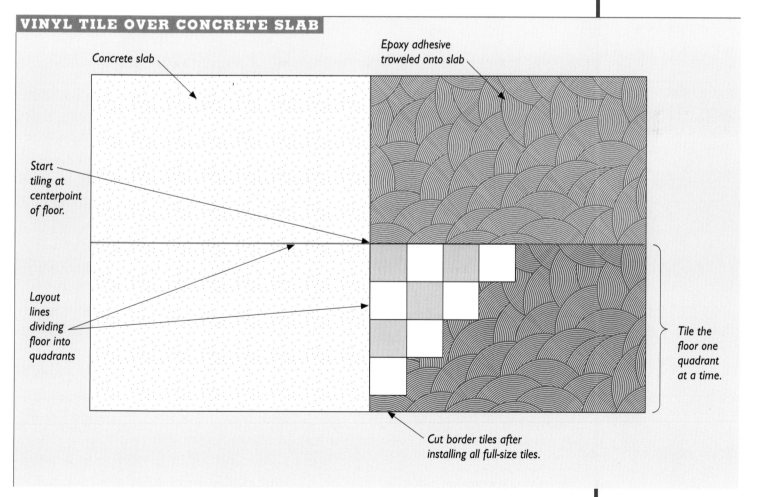

VINYL TILE OVER CONCRETE SLAB

Concrete slab

Epoxy adhesive troweled onto slab

Start tiling at centerpoint of floor.

Layout lines dividing floor into quadrants

Tile the floor one quadrant at a time.

Cut border tiles after installing all full-size tiles.

After troweling down the epoxy, set up a box fan to blow air across the floor and toward an open window. That'll help speed the curing process and vent the epoxy's pungent odor from the room.

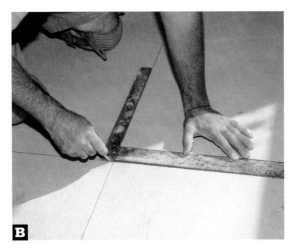

B

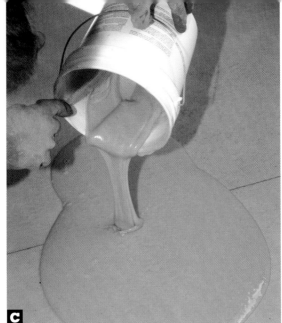

C

with the perpendicular pencil lines. Snap the chalkline to divide the room into quadrants.

4. To ensure you don't lose sight of the two intersecting chalklines, use the framing square and pencil to trace over the entire length of both lines, as shown in **B**.

Apply the epoxy

If you've never before worked with epoxy, there are two things you must know: First, it's critically important to thoroughly mix the two parts together. I know there are other products that state "mix thoroughly before use," but in most cases it doesn't really matter. With epoxy it's all that matters. Failing to thoroughly blend the hardener into the resin will result in a gooey mess, not a long-lasting, super-strong adhesive.

Second, epoxy is a thermosetting adhesive, meaning that the chemical reaction that occurs when you mix together the two parts creates heat that begins the curing process. That's why you typically have very little time to apply epoxy before it starts hardening. Fortunately the epoxy used to set vinyl tile is much more forgiving. It's specially formulated to permit you to work at a leisurely pace. In fact, after applying the epoxy,

you must wait 30 minutes for it to "set up" before you can begin laying tiles.

1. Put on a pair of rubber gloves, then pour the entire contents of the hardener (Part B) into the bucket of epoxy resin (Part A). Use a large wooden paint stirrer to thoroughly mix the two parts together. Stir from the bottom of the bucket all the way to the top; continue mixing for at least five minutes.

2. Once the epoxy is completely blended, pour it out onto the concrete slab, as shown in **C**. Scrape the bucket clean with the wooden stirrer.

3. Spread a very thin, even layer of epoxy across the floor using a 1/16-in.-wide by 1/16-in.-deep notched trowel, as shown in **D**. As you spread the epoxy, be very careful not to miss any spots. It's important to provide 100-percent coverage.

If the area you're tiling is 125 sq. ft. or less, apply epoxy to the entire floor. For larger rooms, apply epoxy to half of the floor, set the tiles, then epoxy the second half.

After applying the epoxy, take a break. You must wait 30 minutes before laying any tile.

D

Start Tiling

After waiting the required 30 minutes for the epoxy to set up, you can begin tiling. Again, the strategy is to tile one quadrant at a time, starting at the center of the room. If you've put epoxy on the whole floor, then you'll need to put down a duck board to walk on—you can't walk directly on the epoxy. A duck board is simply a 2×8 or wider plank with a narrow cleat fastened near each end. The cleats keep the plank up off the floor. Lay the duck board over the epoxied floor, set the first few tiles, then remove the board and stand on the tiles.

Here, we installed an alternating checkerboard pattern using midnight black and charcoal gray tiles. The tiles have flecked pattern lines running across their surfaces. We took the time to align the tiles so that all the black-tile pattern lines ran parallel with the length of the room, and all the gray tiles ran perpendicularly across the width of the room. This alternating right-angle pattern alignment isn't critical, but it does create a more pleasant-looking floor.

Set the first two rows

1. Starting at the exact center of the room, where the two layout lines intersect, install the first tile, as shown in **A**. Be sure the edges of

A

B

the tile align perfectly with the right-angle pencil lines. Firmly press down on the tile to ensure good adhesion with the epoxy.

2. Set the second tile in place, butting it tight against the first tile, as shown in **B**. Install a third tile along the same line.

TRADE SECRET

Before pressing a tile down into the epoxy, check its alignment. If it's not exactly in position, grip one edge with the fingertips of both hands and pull on the tile. It takes a bit of strength, but the tile will slide into position.

PRO TIP

As you take the tiles from their cardboard boxes, carefully inspect each one before pressing it down into the epoxy. Some tiles will have chipped or busted-off corners, especially the tiles located at the very bottom of the box. Set aside the damaged tiles and cut them up for use as border or corner tiles.

3. Now move back to the first tile and start laying tiles in the opposite direction, as shown in **C**. Again, be sure to firmly press down each tile.

Complete the first quadrant

1. Keep tiling in rows, moving across both the length and the width of the room. The most-efficient method is to set three or four tiles in one direction, then switch and set a few in the opposite direction. Be sure to walk only on the tiles, never on the epoxy-coated slab.

2. Continue to install full-size tiles until you've completed the first quadrant, as shown in **D**. Don't worry about stopping to cut tiles to fit along the walls; that'll be done later.

Tile the Second Quadrant

1. Once you've completed the first quadrant, move on to the second quadrant. Again, start at the room center and work out toward the walls, one tile at a time, as shown in **E**.

2. Keep tiling the second quadrant, moving in both directions, until you butt up against the first-quadrant tiles, as shown in **F**.

Finish installing all the full-size tiles in the second quadrant.

Cut the Vinyl Tile

Once you've installed all the full-size tiles in both the first and second quadrants, it's time to cut the border tiles that go around the room perimeter.

You could measure and mark each tile for cutting, but I'll show you the pro technique for

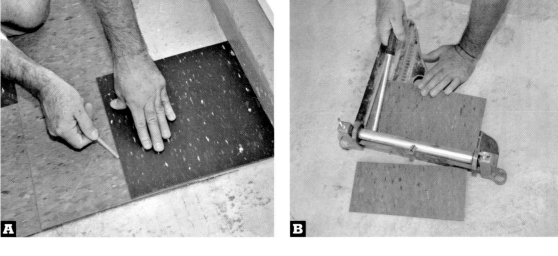

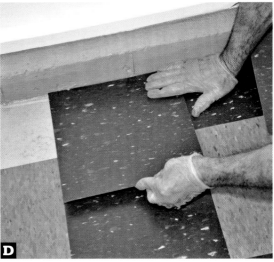

marking tiles. It's quick, easy, highly accurate, and requires no measuring.

Mark and cut border tiles

1. Place the tile to be cut (the border tile) on top of the installed tile that's closest to the wall. Adjust the border tile so that its four edges are perfectly aligned with the installed tile below.

2. Place another tile on top of the border tile and press its edge tight to the wall. Now, draw a line along the edge of the top tile, marking the border tile, as shown in **A**. Remove the border tile.

3. Bring the border tile over to the vinyl tile cutter. Hold the tile in the cutter with its edge pressed against the fence and the pencil line directly under the blade. Pull down on the

cutter's handle to slice the tile in two, as shown in **B**.

4. Set the border tile into place, making sure that the cut edge is positioned against the wall, as shown in **C**. Firmly press the tile down into the epoxy.

Mark and cut corner tiles

When cutting tiles to fit an inside room corner, use the same place-and-trace technique employed for marking the border tiles. In this case, you'll have to mark two cut lines. Here's how:

1. Set the tile to be cut (the corner tile) on top of the installed tile that's closest to the wall. Adjust the corner tile so that it's perfectly aligned with the installed tile below, as shown in **D**.

TRADE SECRET

To ensure a long-lasting, permanent bond with the epoxy, rent a 150-lb. segmented steel roller and make several passes back and forth across the floor. Roll in straight lines across the width and length of the room, and diagonally from corner to corner.

2. Place another tile on top of the corner tile, press it tight to the wall, and draw a line along its edge to mark the corner tile, as shown in **E**.

3. Shift the corner tile to the opposite wall, as shown in **F**. Again, align the corner tile's edges with the tile below.

4. Place a tile on top of the corner tile, press it tight to the wall, and mark the second cut line onto the corner tile, as shown in **G**.

5. Use the vinyl tile cutter to execute both cuts in the corner tile.

6. Set the corner tile into place with the cut edges butting up against the walls, as shown in **H**. Firmly press the tile down into the epoxy.

Complete the Final Quadrants

With half the room completed, you can now tile the third and fourth quadrants. If you had earlier applied epoxy to the entire floor, then you can immediately start tiling and skip Step 1 below. However, if you had only spread epoxy on half of the floor, as we did, then you'll have to repeat all of the steps described for tiling the first two quadrants.

Hot Tip for Notching Vinyl Tiles

AT SOME POINT DURING A VINYL-TILE JOB, you'll have to notch a few tiles to fit around doorways, outside wall corners, and other obstructions. The tiles are incredibly dense and hard, but you can easily slice through them with a sharp utility knife, if you know the secret.

1. Start by using an electric heat gun to warm the tile. Hold the gun's nozzle at least 2 in. from the tile and slowly wave it back and forth across both cut lines, as shown in **A**. Never allow the heat gun to rest in one spot or you'll blister the tile.

2. Apply heat to the tile for approximately 60 seconds, then lay the tile on a flat, hard surface. Use a sharp utility knife to cut out the notch, as shown in **B**.

3. As the tile cools it will become more difficult to cut. If you can't slice cleanly through the second cut line, you can apply more heat and try again, or simply score the cut line and then bend the tile; the notch piece will snap off, as shown in **C**.

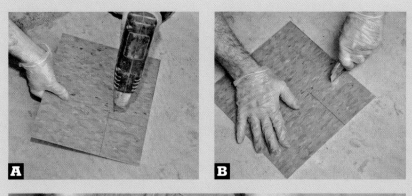

1. Pour the epoxy hardener into the resin and mix with a clean wooden stirring stick. Stir for at least five minutes until the two parts are well blended. Pour the epoxy onto the slab and spread it using a $\frac{1}{16}$-in. notched trowel, as shown in **A**. Wait 30 minutes before proceeding.

2. Install all the full-size tiles in the third quadrant, as shown in **B**. Repeat for the fourth and final quadrant.

3. Once you've installed all the full-size tiles, cut tiles to fit along the walls.

4. Finish up by installing wood baseboard or vinyl cove molding around the room's perimeter.

Vinyl cove molding (baseboard) is available in a wide range of colors, so you can easily find one to match—or contrast—the color of the floor tile. You can adhere the molding to the wall with construction adhesive, but for a better bond, use glue that's specifically formulated for use with vinyl cove molding.

BAMBOO FLOORING

Interest in bamboo flooring has grown exponentially over the past few years, and it's easy to see why. Bamboo is attractive, affordable, durable, available in dozens of colors, and grown and harvested in an environmentally responsible manner. So what's not to like?

Bamboo flooring comes in two basic forms: engineered planks and solid bamboo planks. Engineered bamboo is typically installed using the floating-floor method; the wide planks aren't attached to the subfloor. Tongue-and-groove solid bamboo is installed similarly to traditional hardwood flooring: it's fastened down with nails or staples.

Because floating floors are featured elsewhere in this book (see pp. 34 and 126), here I decided to install a prefinished solid bamboo floor with adhesive and staples. This method is a bit more time-consuming—it takes nearly twice as long as a floating floor—but the result is a beautiful, rock-solid floor. ▶ ▶ ▶

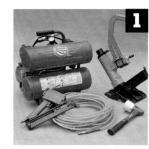

Bamboo contains organic pigments, just as wood does, which will fade slightly when exposed to direct sunlight. Whenever possible, use drapes, blinds, or other window and door treatments to shade the floor from daylight.

Some of the supplies you'll need to install solid bamboo flooring include (left to right): a soft cotton cloth, mineral spirits, urethane wood-flooring adhesive, and a ⅛-in. notched trowel. The cloth and mineral spirits are used to clean off any adhesive that gets onto the prefinished flooring.

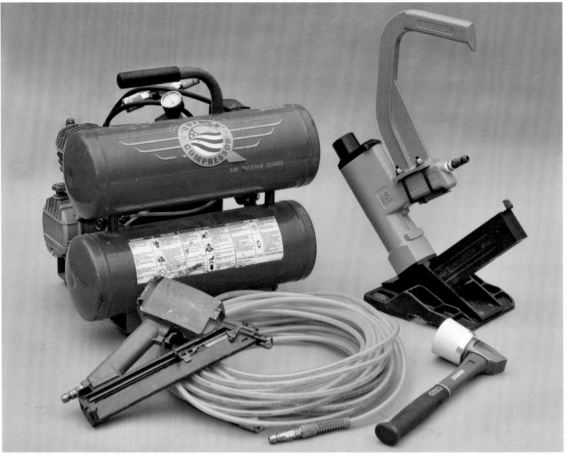

Air force: Installing a solid bamboo floor requires an air compressor, pneumatic finishing nailer, air hose, pneumatic flooring stapler, and a flooring mallet, which comes with the stapler. The finishing nailer is optional and used to face-nail the flooring when there's not enough space to use the stapler. However, you could use a hammer and finishing nails instead.

Tools and Materials

To install solid bamboo flooring you'll need the usual collection of carpentry tools, including a hammer, tape measure, chalk reel, chisel, and power saw. A motorized miter saw is definitely the quickest, easiest way to cut flooring, and it produces the smoothest cuts. However, molding will hide all the cuts, so they don't have to be absolutely perfect; you can also cut the flooring with a portable circular saw, jigsaw, or even a handsaw.

You'll also need some specialty tools and materials, starting with an air compressor and pneumatic flooring stapler. It doesn't make sense to buy these tools, especially if you're only installing floors in one or two rooms, so rent them by the day at a local tool rental dealer. Be sure the stapler can accommodate the thickness of the flooring. The Bostitch® stapler we used had plastic shims that allowed us to adjust the tool's plate to sit perfectly on the edge of the ⅝-in.-thick bamboo planks. If you use an ill-fitting stapler, you'll end up damaging the flooring.

We fastened the planks down with flooring adhesive and 2-in.-long staples. Be aware, however, that not all adhesives are equal. You must use a urethane-based wood-flooring adhesive that's specifically recommended for use with bamboo. We bought a 4-gal. bucket of adhesive and ended up using little more than half of it to install about 120 sq. ft. of flooring.

You'll also have to rent a 90-lb. to 150-lb. steel floor roller. For glue-down installations, the flooring manufacturer recommends rolling the floor to ensure good adhesion. Because we used glue and staples—not just glue—I'm not sure how necessary it was to roll the floor, but we did it anyway just to be safe.

SOLID BAMBOO INSTALLATION

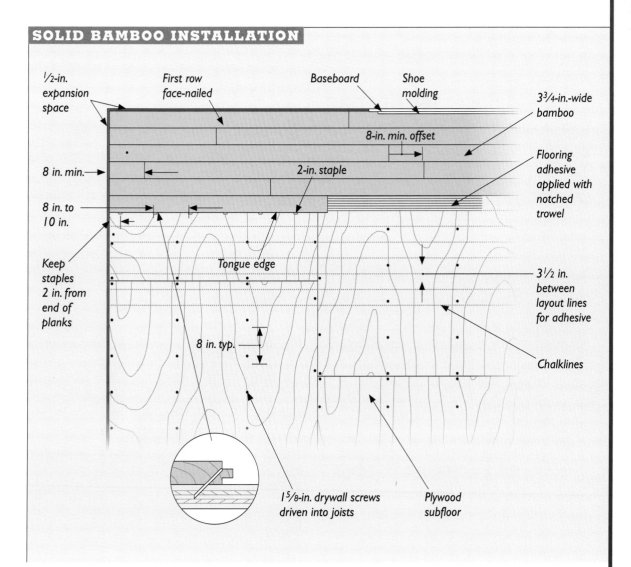

½-in. expansion space

First row face-nailed

Baseboard

Shoe molding

3¾-in.-wide bamboo

8-in. min. offset

8 in. min.

2-in. staple

Flooring adhesive applied with notched trowel

8 in. to 10 in.

Keep staples 2 in. from end of planks

Tongue edge

3½ in. between layout lines for adhesive

8 in. typ.

Chalklines

1⅝-in. drywall screws driven into joists

Plywood subfloor

What Is Bamboo?

BAMBOO LOOKS LIKE WOOD, feels like wood, and cuts like wood. Heck, it even smells like wood. And it's denser than most hardwoods, including maple and oak. But you might be surprised to learn that bamboo isn't wood at all; it's actually grass. And because it's grass, bamboo is one of the fastest-growing plants in the world.

Bamboo can be harvested after just four or five years. By comparison, it typically takes between 30 and 60 years before hardwood trees can be milled into lumber. Plus, a bamboo plant can regenerate itself after cutting and be har-vested again just four or five years later. Try that with an oak tree.

As high demand, short supplies, and soaring prices continue to plague the availability of some hardwoods, bamboo continues to grow—pardon the pun—more and more popular. Besides flooring, bamboo is now available as edge banding, butcherblock countertops, and panels and veneers in sizes up to 4 ft. by 8 ft.

Finally, most bamboo today is grown on regulated, sustainable plantations, making it an environmentally smart building material.

Prep the Room for Flooring

Before installing solid bamboo planks, it's usually necessary to prepare the room by removing the existing flooring. In this case, we had to take up some old wall-to-wall carpeting and rubber padding.

However, if the existing floor is flat, sound, and thin—for example, if it's covered in resilient vinyl tiles or sheets—you can lay the bamboo right over it. Thicker flooring, such as hardwood or engineered planks, will have to be removed because they'll create difficult height transitions between rooms. You can also lay bamboo over thin ceramic tile, but in those situations choose a floating-floor bamboo product, which doesn't get fastened down.

Remove the baseboard molding

Start by removing the baseboard and shoe molding, if there is any, from around the perimeter of the room. If you plan to save the molding and reinstall it later, remove it carefully so as not to crack it.

Also, label each piece so you'll know exactly where it goes. I've found it useful to mark the moldings thusly: North Wall 1, North Wall 2, South Wall 1, and so on. The numbers represent the sequence, from left to right, in which the moldings were installed. This system lets me know exactly where and in what order each piece of molding goes, without having to label the walls as well. Of course, you do have to know north from south.

If the room has shoe molding—ours did not—insert a thin pry bar between the top of the narrow quarter-round molding and the baseboard. Carefully pry the shoe away from the baseboard a little at a time along its entire length. Repeat until the shoe pulls free.

1. Run a sharp utility knife along the top edge of the baseboard molding, as shown in **A**. Use just enough pressure to slice through the paint film. If you skip this step, you run the risk of peeling off wall paint and the paper face of the drywall when you remove the baseboard.

2. Slip a thin pry bar behind the baseboard molding, starting near a corner or at an end

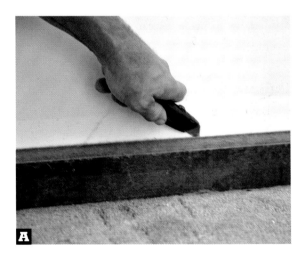

A

B

C

joint between two lengths of molding. Gently pry the molding away from the wall, a little at a time, as shown in **B**. Be careful not to damage the wall, and each time you reposition the pry bar, try to place it near a nail for greater leverage.

Pull up the carpeting

1. Beginning in the corner of the room, slip the hook end of your pry bar behind the carpeting and pull up to lift the carpeting away from the floor, as shown in **C**. Grab the edge of the carpet and yank it away from one wall. If the room is rectangular, pull up the carpet along the shortest wall.

Solid Bamboo Flooring

I ADMIT THAT I WAS A BIT SURPRISED THE FIRST TIME I SAW solid bamboo flooring. The plank was indeed 100-percent solid bamboo, but it wasn't milled from a single board. Instead, each plank was composed of 15 thin, narrow bamboo strips.

The strips are slathered with glue, stacked, and then formed into rough blanks in a large hydraulic press (bottom). The dried blanks are then trimmed, sanded, and milled into tongue-and-groove planks.

Flat-grain, solid-strip bamboo flooring is made up of 15 thin bamboo strips.

The bamboo strips are glued up and pressed together in a hydraulic press.

D

E

G

F

2. Loosely roll the carpeting about 3 ft. or 4 ft. away from the wall. Stop and use a sharp utility knife to slice the carpeting along its entire length into a 2-ft.- to 3-ft.-wide strip, as shown in **D**.

3. Cut the strip of carpeting into large squares, then stack up the squares, as shown in **E**. Roll up another 3 ft. or 4 ft. of carpeting,

then stop, slice it, and cut the strip into squares. Repeat this procedure all the way across the room. The reason I recommend slicing and then cutting up the carpeting is that it's much easier to carry, transport, and discard smaller pieces of carpeting than one large, heavy roll.

Remove the carpet padding

1. Again, starting at the shortest wall, grab the foam-rubber carpet padding and pull it away from the floor. You'll likely find that the padding is stapled down, so try not to rip it.

2. Roll the padding across the floor, as shown in **F**. Unlike carpeting, padding is very lightweight and pliable, so you can remove it all in one big roll.

3. If the padding was stapled down, you'll find small tufts of padding left behind with each staple. It's important to remove these pieces before laying the floor. Use a hammer and slotted screwdriver or thin pry bar to remove each and every staple and bit of padding, as shown in **G**.

Pry up the tack strips

Nailed down around the perimeter of the room you'll find narrow wood strips that are studded by hundreds of tiny, extremely sharp metal points. Called tack strips, these pieces held down the edges of the carpeting. You must remove all the tack strips before proceeding.

1. Use a hammer and thin bar to pry the tack strips from the subfloor, as shown in **H**. Stack them in a neat pile off to one side.

2. Once you've pried up all the tack strips, carry them out of the room.

Screw down the plywood subfloor

With all the old carpeting and padding gone, it's the ideal time to securely screw down the plywood subfloor. This will help eliminate squeaks and any soft, bouncy spots. Take this opportunity to also sand down high spots, repair large holes and cracks, and fill low spots with floor-leveling compound.

When screwing down a plywood subfloor, it's important to drive the screws into the floor joists. To locate the joists, look at the nail pat-

Semi-Automatic Screw Driving

IT'S IMPORTANT TO SCREW DOWN the subfloor to the floor joists prior to installing the bamboo flooring. However, you can cut the time it takes to perform this job in half by using an auto-feed cordless drill/driver. This rapid-fire tool has a magazine that accepts collated strips of drywall screws. Simply load the magazine, squeeze the trigger, and push down to drive a screw. The magazine automatically advances the strip after each screw to move the next screw into position.

An auto-feed drill/driver makes fast work of screwing down the plywood subfloor.

tern on the subfloor. Chances are good that the plywood was nailed to the joists. You can confirm the joist location by driving a 3-in. drywall screw down into the floor. It'll be obvious if you hit the joist or the empty space in between joists.

1. Once you've located a joist, snap a chalkline onto the subfloor indicating the center of the joist, as shown in **I**. Measure over 16 in. to find the next joist, and snap another line. Repeat until you've snapped a line for every joist.

PRO TIP

If you find that screwing down the subfloor with a standard drill/driver causes too much strain and stress on your hand and wrist, switch to a cordless impact driver. This compact brute of a tool has superior power, but uses a combination of high-speed rotation and concussive force to drive screws with virtually no wrist-wrenching torque.

When cutting bamboo planks with a power saw, splintering can occur as the blade exits the cut. Position the plank so the blade cuts into the groove edge first and advances through to the tongue edge. That way, any splintering will occur on the tongue, which will be hidden from view once the flooring is laid.

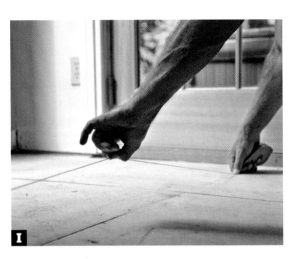

2. Using a drill/driver or impact driver, drive 1⅝-in. drywall screws down through the subfloor and into the joists, as shown in **J**. For maximum effectiveness, space the screws no more than 8 in. apart.

Undercut the door casings

Before the installation can begin, you must check to see if the bamboo flooring will slide underneath the door casings. If not, you'll have to trim the bottom ends of the casings, which is a whole lot easier than notching the flooring around them.

Note that you might also need to trim the doorjambs, but in most cases the flooring butts against the jambs and doesn't slide underneath them. That's because a threshold or transition molding typically hides the joint.

1. If the casings need trimming, start by laying a bamboo plank upside down on the subfloor right next to the casing. (Placing it upside down protects the finished surface from saw scratches.) Lay a flush-cutting saw flat on top of the plank and cut through the casing, as shown in **K**. Remove the severed piece of wood and repeat for the other door casings.

2. Sweep the subfloor clean of all debris, then go over every square inch of the floor with a wet/dry vacuum.

Lay the Starter Rows

With the subfloor prepped it's time to install the bamboo planks. However, before laying the first row of flooring you must find the width of the planks in the last row. That's because the last row needs to be at least 2 in. wide.

Here's how to calculate the width of the last row: Measure the room width, then subtract 1 in. for a ½-in. expansion space at the starting and ending walls. Divide the room width by 3¾ in. (3.75)—the width of each plank—to find the number of rows it'll take to cover the room. For example, if the room is 8 ft. 6 in. wide (102 in.) subtract an inch and divide by 3.75 to get 26.933. That means there will be 26 rows of flooring, and the last row will be 0.933 of one plank wide. Multiply 0.933 times 3.75 to calculate the width of the planks in the last row: 3.498, or 3½ in. If the last row ends up being less than 2 in. wide, you'll have to rip down the planks in the first row.

Next, do a dry run (no glue or staples) by laying out the first three or four rows of flooring. Cut the planks, as necessary, to ensure the end joints are staggered at least 8 in. from one row to the next.

As you cut the last plank in each row, save the cutoff piece to start a row. Discard any cutoff that's less than 8 in. long.

Install the first row

1. Set ½-in.-thick wood spacer blocks along the starting wall, as shown in **A** (see p. 174). Space the blocks about 4 ft. apart; they'll be removed later, leaving behind an expansion gap that will be hidden by the baseboard molding.

2. Set the groove edge of the planks in the first row against the spacer blocks (or the cut edge if you ripped them down). Be sure the tongue edge is facing out into the room. Now measure from the left edge of the first row to the ending wall at the opposite end of the room. Repeat for the right edge. If the two measurements aren't equal, then the first row of flooring isn't parallel with the ending wall.

Sawing Solid Bamboo Flooring

YOU CAN USE VIRTUALLY ANY WOODWORKING SAW to crosscut bamboo planks to length, including a portable circular saw or even a handsaw. However, the two best tools to use are a power miter saw or a portable jigsaw.

A miter saw makes the quickest, smoothest cuts, but it's rather large and produces quite a bit of dust, so it's best to set up the saw outdoors or in a nearby garage. A jigsaw cuts slower and rougher, but its portable size and minimal dust output makes it ideal for use in the room. To make cleanup easier, put down a small drop cloth to catch the dust.

When cutting with a power miter saw, place the plank on the saw table with its finished side facing up (below top). For a jigsaw, hold the plank facedown so that any splintering occurs on the underside (below bottom). Also, guide the jigsaw along a layout square for straight, square cuts.

You can crosscut bamboo flooring with either a power miter saw (above) or a portable jigsaw (left). When using a jigsaw, hold a layout square in place as a straight-edge guide.

Correct a skewed row by slipping thin shims behind one end of the flooring until the two across-the-room measurements are equal. If you don't start with a parallel first row, the last row will have to be cut wider at one end than the other, which is a sign of sloppy workmanship.

3. Use a ⅛-in. notched trowel to spread adhesive onto the subfloor along the length of the starting wall, as shown in **B**.

4. Set the first plank down into the adhesive with its tongue edge facing out, as shown in **C**. Press the plank against the spacer blocks.

5. Use a pneumatic finishing nailer and 2-in. finishing nails to face-nail the first plank to the subfloor, as shown in **D**. Space the nails about 24 in. apart. If you don't have a finishing nailer, fasten the plank using a hammer and 2-in. (6d) finishing nails. Just be sure to drill pilot holes first; bamboo is too hard to simply nail straight through.

6. Slide the second plank into place, making sure the groove on its end fits over the tongue on the end of the first plank. Place a piece of scrapwood against the end of the plank and tap it with a hammer to close the end joint with the first plank. Install the remaining planks in the first row in a similar manner.

D

E

PRO TIP

Wet flooring adhesive can be wiped off tools with mineral spirits, but that's a messy chore. Try this instead: Wait until the next day, after the adhesive has dried to a rubbery film. Then simply scrape it off the tools with a metal putty knife.

7. After installing the last plank in the first row, slip a pry bar over its end and pry it away from the wall to force closed the end joint, as shown in **E**. Then, face-nail the remaining planks in the first row.

Complete the starter rows

1. Using the notched trowel, spread an 8-in.- to 10-in.-wide swath of adhesive onto the subfloor, as shown in **F**. If adhesive gets on the first-row planks, wipe it off immediately with a rag slightly dampened with mineral spirits.

2. Make a tapping block from an 8-in.- to 10-in.-long scrap piece of flooring. Rip the scrap to about 2 in. wide, saving the grooved edge.

Install the planks for the second row by sliding their grooved edge over the protruding tongue on the first row. Put the grooved edge of

F

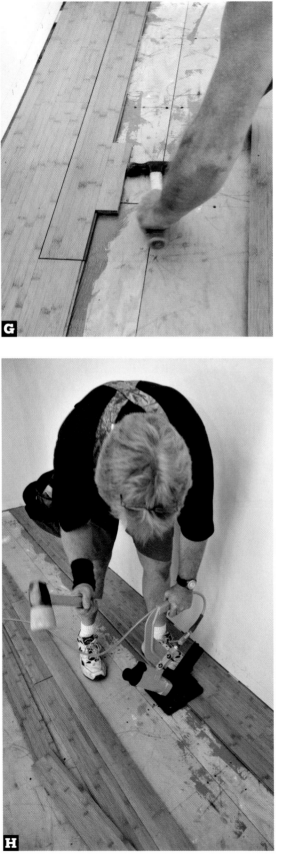

the tapping block over the tongue on the planks
in the second row, and tap on the block's square
edge with a hammer to close the tongue-and-
groove joint between the rows of flooring.

The second row is still too close to the wall
to accommodate the pneumatic flooring stapler,
but don't face-nail it. Instead, drill $\frac{3}{32}$-in.-dia.
pilot holes through the tongue at a 45-degree
angle and hammer in 2-in. (6d) finishing nails.
Use a hammer and nailset to drive the nail heads
below the surface.

3. Install the third-row planks, using a tapping
block and hammer to drive the planks into
place, as shown in **G**.

4. Once you've installed the third row, you
can begin using the pneumatic stapler to
fasten the planks. Set the notch in the stapler's
shoe plate over the square edge of the plank.
Use the mallet to forcefully whack the poppet
actuator, which is the large, round knob
protruding from the top of the stapler, as
shown in **H**. That action will fire one staple at
a precise angle through the tongue and into
the subfloor. Check to be sure the staple is
flush with or slightly below the surface. If necessary, adjust the tool or the compressor's air
pressure.

Continue stapling the planks in the starter
rows, spacing the staples about 8 in. to 10 in. apart.

Continue across the Room

With the starter rows installed, continue to lay
the bamboo planks across the floor. Be sure to
leave $\frac{1}{2}$-in. expansion spaces along all walls,
and always use a hammer and tapping block to
close the tongue-and-groove joints. Hammering
directly onto a plank edge will crush the tongue,

making it difficult—if not impossible—to install the next row of planks.

Install flooring across the room

1. After completing the starter rows, use a chalk reel to snap lines onto the subfloor across the room, as shown in **A**. Space the chalklines 3½ in. apart (the width of a plank).

2. Use a 3-in.-wide notched plastic putty knife to spread adhesive in the space between the flooring and the first chalkline, as shown in **B**. By applying a narrow band of adhesive for each row instead of a wide swath across several square feet, you'll greatly reduce the chance of getting sticky glue all over your tools, hands, clothing, and other surfaces.

Avoiding Split Tongue

WHEN STAPLING DOWN SOLID BAMBOO FLOORING, be sure to keep the staples at least 2 in. away from the ends of the planks. Stapling any closer will surely split the tongue, and then it'll be impossible to install the next row of planks.

If you accidentally staple too close to the end of a plank and splinter the tongue, don't panic. You can usually remedy the situation without ripping out the plank. Start by trying to extract the staple using a thin pry bar and locking pliers. Be careful not to cause any more damage to the tongue or to the plank.

If you can't pull out the staple, slip a close-quarter hacksaw—or just a hacksaw blade—under the plank and saw through the staple. Use pliers to remove the staple head and then, if necessary, use a hammer and nailset to drive the remaining staple legs flush with the subfloor.

Press or tap the split tongue back into position. If the tongue is badly cracked, simply remove the damaged section.

Driving a staple too close to the end of a plank will split the tongue. Keep staples at least 2 in. from the end of a plank. (Photo by Joseph Truini)

A

B

Not-So-Notched Putty Knife

THE NEATEST, MOST EFFECTIVE WAY to spread flooring adhesive is with a plastic 3-in.-wide notched putty knife. However, I noticed that by the end of the day the knife wasn't applying thick, sharply formed ridges of adhesive, which is critical for good adhesion. Upon closer inspection I discovered that the sharp teeth on the knife had been worn down to mere nubs (below left). Be sure to buy two or three extra putty knives (they only cost about a buck apiece) and replace them as soon as they start to show signs of wear.

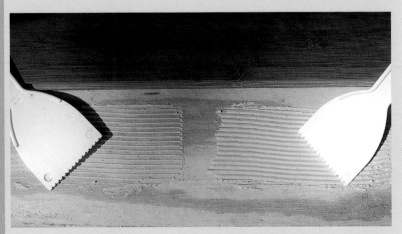

The notched teeth on plastic putty knives will wear down after awhile, preventing you from applying the proper amount of adhesive. A new knife (above right) creates thick, highly defined ridges of adhesive. (Photo by Joseph Truini)

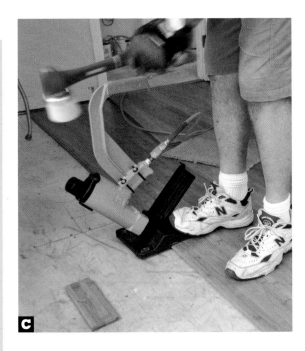

C

D

3. Continue to install planks across the room. For each row, spread adhesive with the 3-in. knife, tap the planks together, then fasten them with the stapler, as shown in **C**.

4. When you get to a doorway, where the bamboo meets another floor, install transition molding. In our case, we concealed the seam between the bamboo and adjacent carpeting with an aluminum transition strip, as shown in **D**.

Finish up

1. As you approach the opposite wall, you'll eventually run out of space to use the pneu-matic stapler and mallet. At that point, fasten the planks in the last two or three rows using a hammer and 2-in. (6d) finishing nails. Drill pilot holes through the tongue at about 45 degrees and then hammer in the nails, being careful not to strike the edge of the plank, as shown in **E**. Use a hammer and nailset to drive the nail heads below the surface.

2. When setting the second-to-last row of planks, there won't be room to use a hammer and tapping block to close the joints. Place a narrow scrap of flooring against the plank, then take a chisel and hammer it into the subfloor very close to the scrap piece. Pull back on the chisel handle to force the plank into position, as shown in **F**. Nail through the tongue to secure the plank.

3. Measure the distance from the wall to the edge of the planks in the second-to-last row. Subtract ½ in. for expansion, then rip planks to that width using a tablesaw (preferred), portable circular saw, or jigsaw. Again, the ripped edges will be hidden by the baseboard molding, so the cuts don't have to be perfect.

Setting Stubborn Staples

WHEN STAPLING DOWN BAMBOO FLOORING, IT'S CRITICALLY important that each staple ends up flush with or just slightly below the surface of the plank's tongue. If not, the protruding head of the staple will make it impossible to tap closed the tongue-and-groove joint on the next row.

After installing a row of planks, take a minute to inspect each staple. If you find one that's not driven down all the way, use a hammer and $\frac{3}{32}$-in. nailset to tap it flush. Place the tip of the nailset on the corner of the staple, directly over one of the staple legs, as shown at right. Then strike the nailset with a hammer. Repeat on the opposite corner of the staple.

This technique might seem a bit tedious, but it's necessary: If you place the nailset in the center of the staple and strike it with a hammer, you'll bend the staple head and the two legs will pop out farther.

Staples standing proud will cause problems. Tap them down flush using a hammer and nailset.

Before bringing in the floor roller, be sure to clean the steel rollers of all dirt, mud, grit, or grime. Otherwise, the heavy rollers will scratch up your brand-new floor.

G

I

H

4. Slip the last row of planks into place and face-nail it as you did the first row.

5. After laying the last plank, remove all the spacer blocks from around the room's perimeter, and then bring in the floor roller. Walk very slowly back and forth across the entire floor several times, as shown in G.

6. If the room has an exterior door, as ours did, trim the door's threshold to length, then tap it into place, as shown in H.

7. Drill and countersink screw holes in the threshold, then fasten it down with 1½-in. screws, as shown in I.

J

K

L

8. Find and mark the stud locations on the walls with small pieces of painter's masking tape, as shown in **J**.

9. Slide the baseboard into position, as shown in **K**. Secure the molding with 2-in. (6d) finishing nails, driven into wall studs.

If you'd like, you could also install quarter-round shoe molding.

The completed floor, as shown in **L**, has a rich grain pattern highlighted by dark blond streaks.

PROTIP

Solid bamboo floors require the same routine maintenance as any wood floor. Sweep or vacuum regularly to remove dust, dirt, and abrasive grit. Mop up spills immediately, and clean the surface regularly with a cleanser specifically designed for prefinished wood floors.

RESOURCES

Alloc®
877-362-5562
www.alloc.com
Manufacturer of laminate flooring

Ambient Bamboo^{SM}
866-710-7070
www.ambientbp.com
Manufacturer of bamboo flooring

American Olean
215-393-2411
www.americanolean.com
Manufacturer of ceramic, natural stone, and porcelain tile

Amtico® International
800-268-4260
www.amtico.com
Manufacturer of resilient vinyl flooring

Anderson® Hardwood Floors
864-833-6250
www.andersonfloors.com
Manufacturer of solid-wood and engineered-wood flooring

Arizona Tile®
480-893-9393
www.arizonatile.com
Manufacturer of porcelain, ceramic, and natural stone tile

Armstrong®
800-233-3823
www.armstrong.com
Manufacturer of resilient vinyl, laminate, solid-wood, engineered-wood, linoleum, and ceramic tile

Bruce® Hardwood Floors
800-233-3823
www.bruce.com
Manufacturer of solid-wood, engineered-wood, and laminate flooring

Build Direct^{SM}
877-631-2845
www.builddirect.com
Online retailer for solid-wood, engineered-wood, laminate, bamboo, cork, resilient vinyl, and natural-stone, porcelain, and ceramic tile

Carlisle Wide Plank Floors^{SM}
800-595-9663
www.wideplankflooring.com
Manufacturer of solid-wood and engineered-wood flooring

Columbia® Flooring
800-654-8796
www.columbiaflooring.com
Manufacturer of solid-wood, engineered-wood, and laminate flooring

Congoleum® Flooring
800-274-3266
www.congoleum.com
Manufacturer of resilient vinyl and laminate flooring

Crossville®
931-484-2110
www.crossvilleinc.com
Manufacturer of porcelain and natural-stone tile

Dupont®
877-438-6824
www.flooring.dupont.com
Manufacturer of laminate flooring

Duro-Design
888-528-8518
www.duro-design.com
Manufacturer of bamboo, cork, solid-wood, and engineered-wood flooring

Expanko®
800-345-6202
www.expanko.com
Manufacturer of cork and rubber flooring

Flexco® Floors
800-633-3151
www.flexcofloors.com
Manufacturer of resilient vinyl and rubber flooring

Flooring America®
www.flooringamerica.com
Installer and retailer of laminate, ceramic tile, solid-wood, and engineered-wood flooring

Florida Tile®
800-352-8453
www.floridatile.com
Manufacturer of ceramic, natural stone, and porcelain tile

Forbo® Linoleum
800-842-7839
www.forbo-flooring.com
Manufacturer of linoleum flooring

Formica® Corporation
800-777-5145
www.formicaflooring.com
Manufacturer of laminate flooring

Franklin Hardwood Floors
203-263-8263
www.franklinwood.com
Installer and retailer of solid-wood and engineered-wood flooring

Globus Cork
718-742-7264
www.corkfloor.com
Manufacturer of cork flooring

Hartco® Hardwood Floors
800-233-3823
www.hartcoflooring.com
Manufacturer of solid-wood, engineered-wood, and laminate flooring

iFloor℠
800-454-3941
www.ifloor.com
Online retailer for solid-wood, engineered-wood, laminate, bamboo, and cork flooring

James Hardie® Building Products
888-542-7343
www.jameshardie.com
Manufacturer of cement backerboard

Kährs International
800-800-5247
www.kahrs.com
Manufacturer of engineered-wood flooring

Lumber Liquidators℠
800-427-3966
www.lumberliquidators.com
Online retailer for solid-wood, engineered-wood, laminate, bamboo, and cork flooring

Lyptus®
800-320-9720
www.lyptus.com
Manufacturer of solid-wood and engineered-wood eucalyptus flooring

Mannington Mills
800-482-9527
www.mannington.com
Manufacturer of resilient vinyl, engineered-wood, porcelain tile, and laminate flooring

Mohawk Flooring
800-266-4295
www.mohawkflooring.com
Manufacturer of solid-wood, laminate, engineered-wood, resilient vinyl, and ceramic tile flooring

National Wood Flooring Association®
800-422-4556
www.nwfa.org
Information on hardwood flooring

North American Laminate Flooring Association℠
202-785-9500
www.nalfa.com
Information on laminate flooring

Nuheat® Industries
800-778-9276
www.nuheat.com
Manufacturer of electric radiant-floor heating systems

Pergo
800-337-3746
www.pergo.com
Manufacturer of premium laminate flooring

Quick-Step®
888-387-9882
www.quick-step.com
Manufacturer of laminate flooring

Resilient Floor Covering Institute
706-882-3833
www.rfci.com
Information on resilient vinyl flooring

Robbins®
800-233-3823
www.robbins.com
Manufacturer of solid-wood and engineered-wood flooring

Shaw Industries®
800-441-7429
www.shawfloors.com
Manufacturer of solid-wood, engineered-wood, laminate, and ceramic, natural stone, and porcelain tile flooring

Tarkett®
877-827-5388
www.tarkettna.com
Manufacturer of resilient vinyl sheet and tile, and laminate

Teragren® Fine Bamboo Flooring
800-929-6333
www.teragren.com
Manufacturer of bamboo flooring, panels, countertops, and veneers

Tile Council of North America
864-646-8453
www.tileusa.com
Information on ceramic and porcelain tile

Ultimate Tool
410-757-8656
www.ulitimatetoolinc.com
Manufacturer of floating-floor installation tools, including tapping blocks, pull bars, and spacers

Wilsonart®
800-710-8846
www.wilsonart.com
Manufacturer of laminate flooring

INDEX